More Praise for *With Liberty and Dividends for All*

"While Thomas Piketty proposes  solution is to pay everyone div mon. Both approaches should I
—**James Boyce, Professor of Ecc**

"In this unprecedented time, Pe is just what's needed to spark a movement."
—**Frances Moore Lappé, author of** *Democracy's Edge*

"Writing from a free-market perspective, I have long been concerned about the radical transformation that is occurring in our society. With this book, Peter Barnes shows how a system of universal dividends can simultaneously undergird a broad middle class and make possible a thriving market economy."
—**Dwight Murphey, author of** *A Shared Market Economy*

"In the last three decades, the wealthy have received most of the benefits of economic growth, with typical workers seeing little or no gains. Barnes's proposal to reverse this process with an equal distribution of income from co-owned wealth is worth serious consideration."
—**Dean Baker, author of** *The End of Loser Liberalism*

"If you're concerned about ever-growing inequality, you must read this book. It brings light to where there's only been heat and points us toward a solution that will work for all."
—**Richard Parker, author of** *The Myth of the Middle Class*

"It takes wisdom to transcend seemingly irreconcilable tensions on the issue of inequality. Peter Barnes's 'simple idea' is grounded in such wisdom."
—**John Fullerton, President, Capital Institute**

"Elegant, powerful, pragmatic, and hopeful. This book will change the debate about what's mine and what's ours."
—**David Morris, cofounder, Institute for Local Self-Reliance**

"In this eloquent and powerful book, Peter Barnes identifies a major step toward a fair and just society. Better, he does so in the tradition of our Founders, who worked hard to ensure that every citizen would enjoy equal access to common sources of well-being."
—**Barry Lynn, author of** *Cornered*

WITH LIBERTY
AND DIVIDENDS
FOR ALL

ALSO BY PETER BARNES

Pawns: The Plight of the Citizen-Soldier

The People's Land: A Reader on Land Reform in the United States (ed.)

Who Owns the Sky? Our Common Assets and the Future of Capitalism

Capitalism 3.0: A Guide to Reclaiming the Commons

Climate Solutions: A Citizen's Guide

WITH LIBERTY AND DIVIDENDS FOR ALL

How to Save Our Middle Class
When Jobs Don't Pay Enough

PETER BARNES

Berrett–Koehler Publishers, Inc.
San Francisco
a BK Currents book

Berrett-Koehler Publishers, Inc.
235 Montgomery Street, Suite 650
San Francisco, CA 94104–2916
Tel: (415) 288–0260   Fax: (415) 362–2512   www.bkconnection.com

Ordering Information
Quantity sales. Special discounts are available on quantity purchases by corporations, associa-
tions, and others. For details, contact the "Special Sales Department" at the Berrett-Koehler
address above.
Individual sales. Berrett-Koehler publications are available through most bookstores. They can
also be ordered directly from Berrett-Koehler: Tel: (800) 929–2929; Fax: (802) 864–7626;
www.bkconnection.com.
Orders for college textbook/course adoption use. Please contact Berrett-Koehler:
Tel: (800) 929–2929; Fax: (802) 864–7626.
Orders by U.S. trade bookstores and wholesalers. Please contact Ingram Publisher Services,
Tel: (800) 509–4887; Fax: (800) 838–1149; E-mail: customer.service@
ingrampublisherservices.com; or visit www.ingrampublisherservices.com/Ordering
for details about electronic ordering.

Berrett-Koehler and the BK logo are registered trademarks of Berrett-Koehler Publishers,
Inc.

Printed in the United States of America
Berrett-Koehler books are printed on long-lasting acid-free paper. When it is available,
we choose paper that has been manufactured by environmentally responsible processes.
These may include using trees grown in sustainable forests, incorporating recycled paper,
minimizing chlorine in bleaching, or recycling the energy produced at the paper mill.

Library of Congress Cataloging-in-Publication Data
Barnes, Peter, 1942-
With liberty and dividends for all : how to save our middle class when
jobs don't pay enough / Peter Barnes. -- First Edition.
    pages cm
Summary: "Journalist and business leader Barnes offers new
understanding of why our middle class is withering and a powerful new
solution for how to restore the middle class, reduce inequality, and make
our economy more fair, prosperous, and sustainable"-- Provided by
publisher.
ISBN 978-1-62656-214-1 (paperback)
1. Middle class--United States--Social conditions. 2. Equality--United
States. 3. Sustainable development--United States. I. Title.
HT690.U6B376 2014
305.5'5090973--dc23
                              2014008285
First Edition
19 18 17 16 15 14   10 9 8 7 6 5 4 3 2 1

Interior design/art: Laura Lind Design   *Editor:* Elissa Rabellino
Cover design: Brad Foltz   *Proofreader:* Henri Bensussen
Credit cover art: iStock.com/peterspiro   *Indexer:* Katherine Stimson
Production service: Linda Jupiter Productions

We hold these truths to be self-evident, that all men are created equal, that they are endowed by their Creator with certain unalienable Rights, that among these are Life, Liberty, and the pursuit of Happiness.

–From the US Declaration of Independence

One Nation under God, indivisible, with liberty and justice for all.

–From the US Pledge of Allegiance

For Jonathan Rowe

CONTENTS

PREFACE

I wrote this book because I'm appalled by the decline of America's middle class and outraged when our leaders mislead us about what we can and can't do to stop it.

That said, I'm not by nature an angry person, and this isn't an angry book. I'm a practical person who has started and led businesses for most of my working life. I want to fix capitalism rather than scuttle it. I therefore take a seasoned and, I hope, reasoned look at how our economy presently distributes income and how it might do so better in the future, without in any way diminishing liberty.

We must face the fact that jobs alone won't sustain a large middle class in the future—there just aren't, and won't be, enough good-paying jobs to do that. This means we need broadly shared streams of *nonlabor* income. The best way to create those streams isn't with taxes; rather, it's with dividends from wealth we own together. Such dividends make political as well as economic sense. They rest on conservative as well as liberal principles and can unite our country rather than divide it.

Dividends of this sort aren't redistribution; they're a way to allocate income fairly in the first place so that there's less need to redistribute later. Nor are they government transfers or private charity. Rather, they're legitimate property income.

Dividends from co-owned wealth won't only halt the decline of our middle class; they'll have ancillary benefits as well. They'll dampen capitalism's overuse of nature and, at the same time, supply enough debt-free purchasing power to keep our economy humming.

Of course, I'm fully aware that just because an idea makes sense doesn't mean it will be adopted. Powerful industries and individuals will fight dividends from co-owned wealth. On top of that, our political system is so dysfunctional right now that it can barely keep our government open, much less fix our economy's deeper flaws. Still, I advance this simple and sensible idea because, while system changes don't happen often, they do happen occasionally. A crisis comes, and suddenly what was once unthinkable becomes not only plausible but necessary. Think back to the 1930s and 1940s if you want reminders.

That doesn't mean we should passively wait for a crisis to hit. Quite the contrary: the crisis of 2008 was wasted because we *didn't* prepare for it beforehand. System change requires work that begins well before the reigning system falters. The time to lay the groundwork for universal dividends, therefore, is now. This book shows why and how.

— 1 —

A Simple Idea

*Every individual is born with legitimate claims
on natural property, or its equivalent.*

—Thomas Paine

We live in complicated times. We have far more problems than solutions, and most of our problems are
wickedly complex. That said, it's sometimes the case that
a simple idea can spark profound changes, much as a
small wind can become a hurricane. This happened with
such ideas as the abolition of slavery, equal justice under
law, universal suffrage, and racial and sexual equality.

1

This book is about another simple idea that could have comparable effects in the twenty-first century. The idea is that all persons have a right to income from wealth we inherit or create together. That right derives from our equality of birth. And the time to implement it has arrived.

Why is this? America today is on the brink of losing its historic vision. From our beginnings we aspired to build a meritocratic middle class, and by the mid-twentieth century we had largely done so. Though millions of Americans remained marginalized, our median income—the income that half of Americans earn more than—was enough for a family to live comfortably on, often with only one wage earner. Further, most Americans assumed that their children would live better than they did—in other words, that our broad middle class would not only survive but expand.

But that's not what happened. As we approached and then entered the twenty-first century, our economy continued to grow, but almost all of its gains flowed to a wealthy few. This disturbing fact has been amply noted by presidents and many others, but what hasn't yet been identified is a remedy that can work.

This book contends that paying dividends from wealth we own together is a practical, market-based way to assure the survival of a large middle class. It can be implemented by electronically wiring dividends to every legal resident, one person, one share. Such a reliable flow of nonlabor income can sustain a large middle class for as long as we have a prosperous economy. What's more, it can *keep* our economy prospering by continuously refreshing consumer demand.

The core of this idea isn't new. Thomas Paine, the patriot who inspired our war of independence from Britain, proposed something quite like it in 1797. And Alaska has been running a version of it since 1980. The main things that would be new are the scale and sources of income.

This old/new idea is ready for prime time for two major reasons. One is the lack of alternatives. Our current fiscal and monetary tools can't sustain a large middle class, nor can increased investment in education, infrastructure, and innovation. None of these old palliatives address the reality that for the foreseeable future, there won't be enough good-paying jobs to maintain a large middle class.

A second reason is the current stalemate in American politics. Solutions to all major problems are trapped in a tug-of-war between advocates of smaller and larger government. Dividends from co-owned wealth bypass that bitter war. They require no new taxes or government programs; once set up, they're purely market-based. And because they send legitimate property income to everyone, they can't help but be popular among voters of all stripes.

Would dividends from co-owned wealth mean the end of capitalism? Not at all. They would mean the end of *winner-take-all* capitalism, our currently dominant version, and the beginning of a more balanced version that respects all members of society, including those not yet born. This better-balanced capitalism—we could call it *everyone-gets-a-share capitalism*—wouldn't solve all our problems, but it would do more than any other potential remedy to preserve our middle class, our democracy, and our planet.

ODDLY ENOUGH, THIS BOOK BEGAN as an idea for a board game. The idea came to me while I was teaching a course at Schumacher College in England. I wanted to make the point that capitalism—that is, a market economy with private property and profit-maximizing corporations— isn't necessarily inconsistent with a healthy planet or an equitable society. I projected a PowerPoint slide of the iconic Monopoly board game and said, "Imagine a game like this, except with slightly different rules. There'd be private property, profit-seeking corporations, winners and losers, but at the same time, nature and the middle class would fend for themselves and flourish."

At the time, I had only an inkling of what those slightly different rules might be, but I had no doubt they could be written. My inspiration was that Monopoly itself had been invented by Quakers to demonstrate the ideas of nineteenth-century American economist Henry George. If I could invent a similar game in which markets respected nature and narrowed the gap between rich and poor, per- haps it could inspire a real-world economy that did the same things. (Alas, Monopoly was later copied, patented, and promoted by Parker Brothers, now Hasbro, as a cel- ebration rather than a critique of capitalism.)

After I returned to the United States, game ideas began circulating in my head. I started making prototypes and testing them with my teenage son and his friends. As the game evolved into more elaborate versions, I realized that a game by itself wasn't enough. I needed to describe the actual economic system the game was seeking to evoke. Ergo, I needed to write a book.

The game itself is still in development. It turns out that it's not as easy to create a game as it is to write a book — the numbers have to be right, the play has to be fast, and many things have to sync. Perhaps one day I'll finish the game, or perhaps someone else will. (I invite game developers to contact me.) But the book I started is finished and in your hands.

———

IT'S IMPORTANT TO DISTINGUISH between *economics* and *our economy*. The terms are often conflated but refer to different things. *Economics* is a body of thought; *our economy* is a system that functions in the real world. As has been said in other contexts, the map is not the territory. Our economic system is real terrain, and economics is a picture of it, necessarily inaccurate and incomplete.

Much has been written about the deficiencies of contemporary economics. I'm more concerned about the defects of our actual economy. But to understand those defects — and to fix them — we must start with a sufficiently wide lens, which is why conventional economics is a problem. It obscures what needs to be seen and thereby inhibits us from changing what needs to be changed.

Our economy today is a huge and complex system. As such, it's subject to patterns of behavior that characterize other complex systems. It's also, like every other system in the universe, part of several larger systems. How you see it depends on where you stand and how wide your lens is. You see it differently if you zoom in on a single part of the system, zoom out to the system as a whole, or zoom out even farther to the larger systems in which our economy is nested.

Many economists view our economy as a self-contained whole. They know it's affected by our society and planet — and conversely, that it *affects* our society and planet — but the impacts in both directions are hard to quantify. It's a lot easier not to count or consider them.

In this book I approach our economy as *both* a self-contained system and part of two larger systems, American society and the biosphere. Viewing it as a part of these larger systems enables us to see how it's out of harmony with both of them, as well as how it might be brought into harmony. Viewing our economy as a self-contained system lets us see how the interactions between its internal parts drive its overall behavior — and how small changes in the structure of those interactions can trigger big changes in aggregate outcomes.

I also adopt a wider-than-conventional view of the *purpose* of an economy. Most economists believe that ever-increasing production is the principal, if not the only, goal of an economy, because if we produce enough stuff, everything else will sort itself out. This mode of thinking made sense in the days when we lacked material goods. Those days, however, are over. Our current surplus production capacity demands two higher purposes for our economy:

ensuring the security of a large middle class and synchronizing human activity with nature. Neither of these objectives arises automatically from producing more stuff. Unless they're consciously built into our economy's structure, we're highly unlikely to achieve them.

WHILE I PROPOSE TO EXPAND THE GOALS of our economy, I don't propose to alter the means by which it achieves them. I wish to be very clear about that. As an entrepreneur, I strongly believe in markets, though markets with more players than today's. And I believe just as strongly in private property, tempered by a certain amount of community property. My ideal economy is a multistakeholder equilibrium in which profit-driven businesses, a large middle class, and the earth's vital ecosystems — acting through legally empowered agents — balance each other for the good of all.

I'm not sure where these beliefs place me on the political spectrum; I draw from economists and politicians of several persuasions. Still, if I had to pick a single thinker who most inspired this book, it would be the American essayist Thomas Paine.

Paine led an extraordinary life. Unlike other Founding Fathers, he wasn't a man of privilege. He was born in England to a Quaker corset maker and sailed, penniless, to Philadelphia five months before the Concord Minutemen fired "the shot heard 'round the world." He then wrote *Common Sense*, the best-selling pamphlet that inspired America to declare independence from his native country. Still impoverished after independence, he returned to England and was charged with libel against the king. Fleeing to France, he was elected to the revolutionary convention despite speaking no French. He narrowly escaped execution twice: once by William Pitt's writ, then by Robespierre's. Returning to America, he died in New Rochelle, New York, in 1809, largely forgotten.

Thomas Paine (1737–1809)

(Portrait by Auguste Milliere, 1880, National Portrait Gallery)

After *Common Sense*, Paine's most famous essays were *The American Crisis* ("These are the times that try men's souls"), *The Rights of Man*, and *The Age of Reason*. His last great work was *Agrarian Justice*, which, despite its title, isn't about agriculture but about property rights.

"There are two kinds of property," Paine contended. "Firstly, natural property, or that which comes to us from the Creator of the universe — such as the earth, air, water. Secondly, artificial or acquired property — the invention of men." The latter kind of property must necessarily be distributed unequally, but the first kind rightfully belonged to everyone equally, Paine thought. It was the "legitimate birthright" of every man and woman, "not charity but a right."

Paine's genius was to invent a way to distribute income from shared ownership of natural property. He proposed a "National Fund" to pay every man and woman fifteen pounds at age twenty-one and ten pounds a year after age fifty-five. (These sums are roughly equal to $17,500 and $11,667, respectively, today.[1]) Revenue for the fund would come from "ground rent" paid by landowners, the privatizers of natural wealth. Paine even showed mathematically how this could work.

Presciently, Paine recognized that land, air, and water could be monetized, not just for the benefit of a few but for the good of all. Further, he saw that this could be done at a national level. This was a remarkable feat of analysis and imagining. If that's Paineism, then call me a Paineist.

─────────

BEFORE WE GET TO THE HEART OF THE BOOK, let me introduce a few key terms.

Dividends are periodic payments made by corporations, mutual funds, or trusts to their shareholders or beneficiaries. Such payments vary from time to time, depending on the earnings of the payers, but at any given time they're the same for each share.

In capitalist economies, dividends are a major form of nonlabor income. To receive them, you must have a legal *right* to receive them. At present, most of those rights are held by a small minority. But there is no reason why ownership of such rights can't be expanded, and good reason why they should be.

Systems—which is to say, conglomerations of parts that continuously interact—are what maintain order throughout our universe, and we should be grateful for that. For purposes of this book, the two most important things to remember are: (1) a system as a whole is distinct from, and greater than, the sum of its parts; and (2) a system's structure determines its outcomes.

Our economy, obviously, is a highly complex system, and making sense of it is never easy, even for economists. But patterns common to all systems tell us, or at least strongly suggest, that wealth distribution within an economy depends more on the design of the system than on the efforts of its individual participants. If a roulette wheel has eighteen black pockets, eighteen red ones, and two green ones, balls will land in the green pockets roughly two thirty-eighths of the time no matter how we throw them. That's why the house always wins. Similarly, if an economic system is structured to distribute income in a certain way, that's what it will do. No matter what we *want* it to do, that's what it *will* do.

The middle class is the group of households sandwiched between the lap of luxury and the yaw of poverty. Though the actual term wasn't used until the mid-nineteenth century, Americans have long believed that it's hugely important for such a class to be as large, prosperous, and secure as possible. The current reality, however, is that our middle class is in steady decline and there's no end

in sight. The old props for sustaining it—public education, labor unions, and economic growth—aren't working anymore. New props are needed, but no one knows
what they are.

Co-owned wealth is the underappreciated complement to
privately owned wealth. It consists of assets created not
by individuals or corporations but by nature or society
as a whole. This little-noticed cornucopia includes our
atmosphere and ecosystems, our sciences and technologies, our legal and financial systems, and the value that
arises from our economic system itself. Such co-owned
wealth is hugely valuable but at the moment is barely
recognized.

To heighten our awareness of co-owned wealth, I use
the adjective *our* in places you might not expect. For example, instead of *the* atmosphere I say *our* atmosphere,
and instead of *the* money supply I say *our* money supply. Using an impersonal article implies that co-owned
wealth belongs to no one. I prefer to speak as if it belongs
to everyone.

Rent is one of the most important and underused concepts in economics. As I (and most economists) use the
term, rent is the money paid to businesses over and above
their costs of labor and capital in competitive markets. It
includes premiums paid for scarce things and excessive
profits extracted by monopolies, oligopolies, and industries coddled by government. As I (but few economists)
also use the term, rent is, in addition to the above, a potentially virtuous flow of money paid to all of us for use

of our co-owned wealth. (See chapters 4 and 5 for a detailed discussion of rent.)

Rent isn't talked about much in polite society; it's the eight-hundred-pound gorilla that everyone pretends isn't there. Economists in particular rarely mention it, not out of ignorance but because they find it awkward to offend those who extract it disproportionately. The time has come, though, to bring rent out of the closet, for it holds the key to saving our middle class and planet.

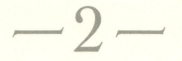

The Tragedy of
Our Middle Class

They're closing down the textile mill across the railroad tracks,
Foreman says these jobs are going, boys,
and they ain't comin' back . . .

—Bruce Springsteen

In 2011, Occupy Wall Street brought to the fore a truth that many had known but few had spoken of: a hugely disproportionate share of wealth in America is concentrated in the hands of the top 1 percent. This thin upper crust currently owns 35 percent of all wealth, while the next 19 percent claims 53 percent. This leaves the

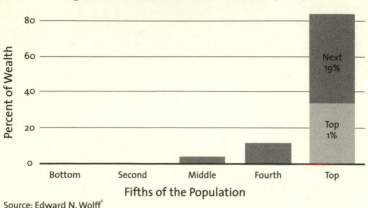

Figure 2.1: US WEALTH DISTRIBUTION (2010)

Source: Edward N. Wolff²

remaining 80 percent of Americans with—well, not much as shown in figure 2.1.

Anyone looking at this graph can't help but ask, "Where's the middle?" It simply isn't there. This isn't the kind of society most Americans want, yet it's what we now have.

This sort of society has two major problems. One is the vastness of the inequality, which has numerous negative side effects. As studies have shown, highly unequal societies have more homicides, obesity, heart disease, mental illness, drug abuse, infant mortality, and teenage pregnancies than do more egalitarian societies.² Highly unequal societies also suffer from a loss of spirit. When people know their economic system is stacked against them, they cease to believe they can attain security and comfort, much less riches. They also lose faith in their political system, which, mirroring their economy, makes a mockery of the American vision.

The second major problem is that while incomes of the rich have soared, incomes of the middle class have declined. According to the 2010 US Census, the median household income fell 8 percent in the last decade. More tellingly, since 1970, the incomes of men in their twenties and early thirties have fallen by 30 percent.[3]

This is historically new. When I was growing up, middle-class families with one breadwinner could send their children to college without incurring huge debts. Wages were rising, housing and education were affordable, and health insurance was within reach. Those days are gone now, and today's middle class is as anxious about its future as my parents were hopeful.

AMERICA'S FOUNDERS ARE REMEMBERED for many things, but one of their greatest inventions is often forgotten: the mass middle class. "The class of citizens who provide at once their own food and their own raiment may be viewed as the most truly independent and happy," wrote James Madison.[4] "They are also the best basis of public liberty and the strongest bulwark of public safety. The greater the proportion of this class to the whole society, the more free, the more independent, and the more happy must be the society itself."

With this vision in mind, one state after another abolished primogeniture, the feudal system under which eldest sons inherited all of their parents' land, while early Congresses reserved land in every new town for universal public education. Thirty years later, the French sociologist Alexis de Tocqueville observed in America "a democratic people, where there is no hereditary wealth, every man works to earn a living; labor is held in honor; the prejudice is not against but in its favor."[5]

Things changed with industrialization, immigration, and the robber barons. A large class of factory workers arose in the cities. They earned pitiful wages, toiled sixty hours a week, and lived in squalid, overcrowded tenements. But they joined unions, and after half a century of struggle, those unions lifted wages, reduced working hours, and helped make housing and higher education affordable for the majority. Thus was born the world's first mass middle class, a fulfillment of the Founders' vision in a postagrarian economy.

The quarter century after World War II was the golden age of America's middle class. Twenty million veterans went to college or bought homes thanks to the GI Bill. Green-lawned suburbs sprouted like mushrooms after rain. Families filled their garages with cars, tools, and barbecues. In 1980, Ronald Reagan proclaimed that it was "morning in America," and most voters believed him, or wanted to.

In fact, it was already after noon, though few realized it at the time. Like agriculture before it, manufacturing had begun shedding workers. Not only were foreign manufacturers outcompeting ours; American companies were moving factories overseas. Americans were told not to worry—we'd become a service economy, and white-collar jobs would fill the blue-collar void. But food servers, retail clerks, and health aides were paid considerably less than their industrial counterparts. A steadily tightening squeeze, with wages stagnating and prices of middle-class necessities rising, took hold.

In addition to deindustrialization, three other long-term phenomena gained momentum after 1980: globalization, automation, and deunionization.

Globalization. Since the early 1800s, economists have argued that trade is good and more trade is better. Their rationale is the theory of comparative advantage. As David Ricardo reasoned, if England could make textiles more efficiently than Portugal, and Portugal could make wine more efficiently than England, then both countries—including their workers—would benefit by trading woolens for port.

But trading in physical goods is one thing and globalization is something else: it is the integration of separate national economies into a single world economy. In any capitalist economy, products are made wherever costs are lowest and sold wherever prices are highest. When the economy is local or national, businesses have some incentive to support the general good—to pay taxes, train workers, contribute to their communities, and so on. But when corporations can scour the planet for the lowest costs and avoid contributing to *any* community, that is no longer true. The big winners, then, are corporate owners, and the big losers are workers and communities.

Automation. When Henry Ford launched the Ford Motor Company in 1903, cars were built by skilled craftsmen one at a time. Ford had many technical patents, but his most revolutionary invention was the assembly line. Within five years he was making one Model T every ninety-eight minutes. By 1929 his River Rouge plant was turning out a car every ten seconds.

The fear of eighteenth-century English weavers was that textile machinery would put them out of work. And it did. What Ford showed in the twentieth century was that automation could have the opposite effect. By making complex products so cheap that millions could afford to buy them, it vastly increased the number of workers needed. On top of that, it enabled large, automated companies to pay decent wages. This was the beginning of industrial America's mass middle class.

Today, automation is displacing workers again. ATMs replace human tellers, e-mail replaces postal workers, computerized trading replaces floor traders, and so on. The result is an American workforce that's splitting into well-paid elites at the top and low-paid service workers at the bottom, with few decently paid punters in the middle.

Deunionization. An affluent economy is a prerequisite for a large middle class but by no means a guarantee. To sustain a large middle class, a nation must consciously and continuously temper the natural impulse of capitalism to minimize labor costs. That has been done by various countries in various ways, but there's always pushback and never a guarantee that gains for the middle class will endure.

Sustaining a large middle class requires counter-balancing the profit-maximizing imperative of corporations. For much of the twentieth century, the requisite counterforce came from labor unions. In the United States and Western Europe, labor unions finished the job that Henry Ford started. Through collective bargaining, they drove up wages and shortened the workweek; through political power, they won such benefits as unemployment insurance and Medicare. In countries like Germany and Sweden, where labor unions have remained strong, so has the middle class. In the United States, by contrast, union membership peaked in 1945 at 35 percent of nonagricultural workers, then started declining. It's now at 12 percent of the total workforce and just 6 percent of private sector workers, and the trend isn't likely to reverse.[6]

THESE THREE PHENOMENA, though distinct, aren't unconnected. They all result from the dominant corporate imperative to maximize profit. And as figure 2.2 shows, they've all shifted money from the middle of our economic ladder to the very top.[7]

Americans were surprisingly slow to notice that the golden era of the middle class had passed. As former Labor Secretary Robert Reich has explained, three factors masked the middle class's descent. First, women entered the labor force in large numbers, providing two incomes for many households. Second, many Americans

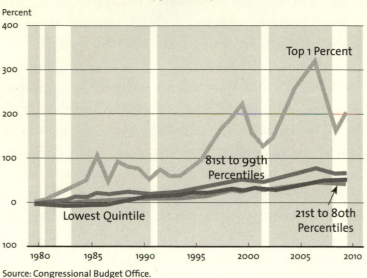

Figure 2.2: THE RICH GET RICHER
(1980–2010)

Source: Congressional Budget Office.

made ends meet, or tried to, by working overtime and taking second jobs. And third, middle-class families maintained their lifestyles thanks to a vast expansion of consumer debt. But these masks couldn't last forever. When the credit bubble burst in 2008, so did the accompanying illusions.[8]

All this is a tragedy not just for hard-hit families but also for the idea of America as a nation of self-reliant citizens. And the tragedy is far from over. According to a recent study, three-quarters of Americans nearing retirement have less than $30,000 in retirement savings.[9] Even with Social Security, they'll end their lives in trailer homes. On top of this, millions of today's twentysomethings will be saddled for decades with student loans they can't repay.

———————

THE DECLINE OF THE MIDDLE CLASS is now in full view, and Americans are hungry for solutions. But what are they? With much fanfare, President Barack Obama in 2009 created the White House Task Force on the Middle Class, headed by Vice President Joe Biden, to find some. The task force dutifully held hearings, consulted experts, and published reports. To no one's great surprise, the reports recommended more education, job training, child care, "green jobs," retirement savings, and other piecemeal measures. Most would be beneficial as far as they went, but they wouldn't go very far, and they certainly wouldn't fix the causes of middle-class decline.

Republicans, meanwhile, have been calling for more tax and spending cuts, deregulation of business, and privatization of Social Security and Medicare. It's not immediately obvious how such policies would strengthen the middle class, but Republicans insist that they would. They argue that unburdened "job creators" would generate rising incomes for all, without unions or higher minimum wage laws. It could happen, I suppose, but I wouldn't bet on it. Far more likely is that wealth would flow upward at an even faster rate.

Think tanks have been busy, too, cranking out papers with lots of bullet points. Mostly, these papers revamp policies that worked a few decades ago. But as financial prospectuses are required to say, "Past performance is no guarantee of future results." Indeed, in history, the way forward is rarely the way back.

Here are the four most-touted pro-middle-class policies and the reasons why they won't halt the current decline:

Stimulus. Though they quarrel over details, most economists agree that when recession strikes, government should rekindle the economy by adding money to it. Democrats prefer to do this through direct spending, Republicans through tax cuts. The Federal Reserve often plays along by lowering interest rates or printing money through a process called "quantitative easing."

Such fiscal and monetary pump-priming often perks up the economy for a while, but it doesn't fix the causes of middle-class decline. As we're seeing nowadays, it's easy for GDP and corporate profits to grow without more income flowing to the middle class.

Job creation. Listen to any politician and you'll hear bold promises to spur job creation. The underlying premise is that more private sector jobs will save the middle class and that given enough incentives, profit-seeking entrepreneurs will create them.

There's no question that the middle class needs jobs. But it doesn't follow that jobs by themselves can sustain a large middle class in the future. Most jobs today pay barely enough to make ends meet. What a large middle class needs is *good-paying* jobs in large numbers, and those simply aren't being created.

In the heyday of America's middle class, jobs at IBM and General Motors were often jobs for life. Employers offered health insurance, paid vacations, and good pensions. Workers' pay and responsibilities tended to rise with seniority. In today's globalized economy, by contrast, good wages and long-term relationships are rare. Workers are expendable—often they're literally "temps"—and their benefits are shrinking. And that's unlikely to change.

It's also unlikely that jobs of the future will pay more than today's (adjusted for inflation). In unionized industries like autos and airlines, two-tier contracts are now the norm. This means that younger workers get paid substantially less than older ones for doing the same work.

Nor is the picture brighter in other industries. Figure 2.3 shows the US Labor Department's list of the ten fastest-growing occupations.[10]

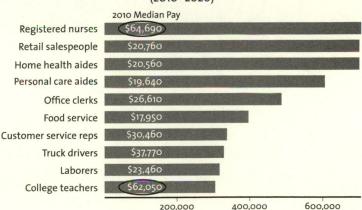

Figure 2.3: TOP TEN GROWTH OCCUPATIONS
(2010–2020)

2010 Median Pay

Occupation	2010 Median Pay
Registered nurses	$64,690
Retail salespeople	$20,760
Home health aides	$20,560
Personal care aides	$19,640
Office clerks	$26,610
Food service	$17,950
Customer service reps	$30,460
Truck drivers	$37,770
Laborers	$23,460
College teachers	$62,050

200,000   400,000   600,000

What these numbers tell us is that the middle class in 2020 will consist largely of nurses and teachers. Never mind that these occupations depend in one way or another on public funding, which nowadays is shrinking. The deeper question that leaps from these numbers is: Where are the millions of good-paying private sector jobs that are needed to sustain a large middle class? The Labor Department doesn't say. Nor does anyone else.

Education. About a year before the financial meltdown, President George W. Bush told a friendly Wall Street audience, "Income inequality is real—it's been rising for more than twenty-five years. And the reason is clear: we have an economy that increasingly rewards education and skills because of that education."[11] The solution, he argued, was for young people to study harder and schools to teach better.

Education—by which I mean both academic and vocational—is a worthy endeavor in its own right, so there's every reason for America to invest more in it than we now do. But we mustn't delude ourselves into thinking that education will cure inequality or sustain a large middle class. It won't.

The reason is simple though not immediately obvious. While it's true that people with college degrees earn more than people without them, it doesn't follow that cranking out college graduates creates more high-paying jobs. It's a logical fallacy, called the *fallacy of composition*, that what works for a few will work for all. Increasing the supply of college grads doesn't increase the demand or the pay rate for them. It gives us better-educated taxi drivers, salespeople, and carpenters, but not better-paid ones. As economist Lawrence Mishel has written, "Boosting college graduations will not materially address either past or future inequalities. In fact, it will exacerbate the already deteriorating pay and benefits facing young college graduates and lead to falling wages among all college graduates."[12]

The same is true for job training. As economic historian Joyce Appleby has observed, "It is true that there are businesses that require labor and individuals who would like jobs but don't qualify for them. And it is true that job training can help. But it doesn't follow that job training programs reduce unemployment or poverty. The reason is that poverty and unemployment are not much influenced by the qualifications of the workforce. They depend, rather, on the demand for labor."[13]

Innovation. American companies love to innovate, and they do it very well. That leads to clever new products and more efficient production processes, but it doesn't lead to more good-paying jobs. In fact, it may lead to fewer.

Consider Apple, the world's most valuable company and exemplar of American ingenuity. Apple's brilliant products are designed in Silicon Valley but made almost entirely in China. What's more, Foxconn, Apple's low-wage Chinese manufacturer (and also Dell's, Hewlett-Packard's, and Intel's), has broken ground on a new factory to make robots. Its goal is to "hire" one million ro-

bots, displacing hundreds of thousands of Chinese workers. "Robots don't complain, or demand higher wages, or
kill themselves," the *Economist* noted wryly.[14]

Then there's Apple's neighbor Google, which along
with its online services is developing a driverless car. If
it catches on, it will be an awesome innovation, but not
one that cab or truck drivers will like. Will FedEx stick
with humans when mechanical drivers are a fraction of
the cost? Not likely.

And what are we to make of the "insourcing" of
manufacturing jobs that has recently raised hopes in the
Midwest? North Canton, Ohio, for example, used to be
home to the Hoover Vacuum Cleaner company, which
once employed seven thousand people there. By 2007,
Hoover had closed all its US factories and moved them
to Mexico and China. It was therefore big news in North
Canton when a company called Suarez Industries an-
nounced that it was moving a heater factory there from
China, seemingly reversing the direction of globalization.

Unfortunately, Suarez needs only 250 local workers
to churn out 10,000 heaters a week. How can they do
that? "We reengineered the Chinese heater," the production manager explained. The Chinese model had 192
screws; the revamped model has 31. So yes, thanks to
innovation, some manufacturing jobs are returning to
America, but they aren't many, and they don't pay well.
When Hoover left town, it was paying assembly-line
workers $13 to $17 an hour. Suarez will pay its screw
turners the minimum wage, $7.85 an hour as this is
written.[15]

If stimulus, job creation, education, and innovation — helpful as they may be — can't sustain a large middle class in the twenty-first century, we'd better do some deep rethinking. And that means digging into all the sources of income within capitalism.

———

BROADLY SPEAKING, CAPITALISM CREATES two kinds of income. One is derived from physical or mental labor, the other from ownership of property rights. At this moment, the middle class gets nearly all of its income from labor. (I'm counting Social Security and pensions as deferred wages and salaries.) By contrast, the top 1 percent reaps the bulk of our economy's capital gains, dividends, and other forms of property income, which not coincidentally are taxed at lower rates than labor income. This arrangement works nicely for the rich but not so nicely for workers whose wages are being squeezed.

The question that needs to be asked is this: From where might the middle class get some nonlabor income? As far as I can tell, almost no one is asking this question today. The unchallenged assumption is that nonlabor income is fine for the top few percent, but everyone else should toil to make ends meet.

To be clear: I'm not saying that nonlabor income should be the primary source of income for most people; I'm saying that it should be a supplement. The rich would still get most of their income from property, and everyone else would still get the bulk of their income from working. But everyone should also get *some* non-labor income as a birthright. Otherwise, we can kiss our large middle class goodbye.

Fix the System,
Not the Symptoms

*A system is a set of things interconnected in such a way that they
produce their own pattern of behavior over time.*

—Donella Meadows

In the previous chapter, I linked the decline of our middle
class to a convergence of historic trends. What I didn't
do was ask whether those trends were mere accidents or
the result of something deeper. In this chapter, I argue
that it's the structure of our economic system that, day
after day, shifts wealth from the middle to the top. This

means that if we want wealth to spread more evenly, we need to change our economic system.

Americans aren't in the habit of thinking, much less acting, systemically; we prefer breaking problems into discrete pieces. Our government agencies, academic disciplines, and nonprofit organizations all focus on specific silos of interest. They develop policies for housing, education, the environment, and so on, but treat our economic system itself—in which every silo affects every other—as off-limits. Wealth distribution is a particularly systemic phenomenon, a result of how all parts of our economy interact. It can't be understood without viewing it at that level, nor can it be fixed without treating it at that level.

The Italian economist Vilfredo Pareto was among the first to notice that *something* in modern economies consistently concentrates wealth at the top. Early in the twentieth century, he observed that about 20 percent of the people in Italy owned about 80 percent of the land.[1] Looking further, he saw the same pattern throughout Europe. This led him to posit that in market economies, about 20 percent of the people will always acquire about 80 percent of the wealth . . . because *that's how market economies work*.

Pareto's formula wasn't purely random; it reflects what mathematicians call a *power law*, meaning a curve that's exponentially skewed to one end, as depicted in figure 3.1. The alternative to a power law is a *bell curve*, which has a large middle with small tails on both ends. What Pareto noticed was that in untempered market

Figure 3.1: POWER CURVE SHOWING 80/20 RULE

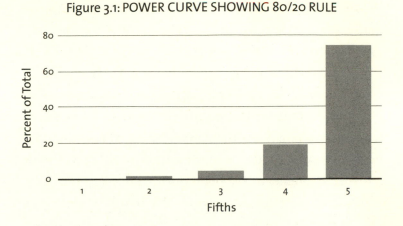

economies, wealth distribution follows a power law rather than a bell curve. A century later, this thesis seems as valid as ever: the 80/20 rule understates wealth concentration in the United States today. (Compare figure 3.1 with figure 2.1.)

Pareto didn't say *why* the 80/20 rule governed wealth distribution; he just noted (to his dismay) that it seemed to do so. In 1992, two American mathematicians, Joshua Epstein and Robert Axtell, dug deeper. Using technology unavailable to Pareto, they built a computer simulation of a market economy (which they called Sugarscape) to see what properties—including inequality—emerged when it ran.[2]

Sugarscape begins by randomly populating a sugar-laden field with sugar-seeking agents. Like humans, the agents have a random distribution of abilities—for example, some see farther or have more energy than others. Every time the computer recalculates, the agents search for sugar as far as their vision allows, then move to the densest sugar they see (burning sugar as they go), and eat the sugar when they get there.

Sugar, of course, is a proxy for wealth. To track wealth distribution, the computer calculates the amount of sugar each agent has accumulated after every move and, on that basis, sorts them into deciles. When the game begins, the distribution of wealth is like a bell curve with a few rich agents, a few poor ones, and a large middle. As the game progresses, however, the middle shrinks and wealth concentrates. By the end of the game, the distribution of wealth is as Pareto's law predicts.

Why is this? Epstein and Axtell tested various hypotheses. One is that wealth distribution correlates with the sugar densities (i.e., the natural wealth) where agents are born. Another is that it mirrors agents' genetic endowments. It turns out that both of these hypotheses are wrong. If the ending distribution of wealth were linked to the random, hence fairly even, distributions of birth location or endowments, wealth distribution would be fairly even as well, and there'd be a permanently large middle class. The reason why wealth concentrates 80/20 is that *every time the system recalculates, it amplifies small differences*.

It's important to note that this amplification doesn't just happen once or even occasionally—it's continuous. As a result, inequality spirals upward thanks to self-reinforcing feedback. Absent any countervailing feedback, differences that start small become ever wider over time.

When you stop and think about it, this isn't a startling discovery. We all know that money begets money and that, relatively speaking, the rich get richer while the poor get poorer. And we understand that this happens because the rich use their initial advantages — money, education, and connections — to gain even more advantages. We also know that because money has the loudest voice in politics, the willingness of government to tax the rich wanes as their wealth waxes, a process that tax-reform advocate Chuck Collins calls the "inequality death spiral."[3]

Though not startling, Epstein and Axtell's finding is nevertheless sobering. It means that small initial differences, such as those in a bell curve, are inexorably magnified until they become extreme differences, such as those in a power law. Which means that, over time, our economic system will necessarily create a small upper crust and a shrunken middle.

This is a crucial point. We know that people have different capacities and drives. Some are smarter than others, and some work harder. But those different abilities don't explain the far greater differences in rewards. Rather, extreme reward differences are driven by the compounding effects of our winner-take-all economy.

If extreme inequality is a built-in property of our present economic system, we've got some deep thinking to do. For this means that even if we educated our children till the cows came home, inspired or cajoled them to work harder, and got them all jobs, we wouldn't sustain a large middle class over time. Upward income flow would remain self-reinforcing, ending only when the system crashed (and maybe not even then, as 2008 showed). The only way to get a less unequal outcome is to build some equalizing flows into the system.

———————

WHEN SYSTEMIC CHANGES ARE PROPOSED in the United States, there are two directions they can go: toward greater government or less. Typically, the former means more regulating, taxing, and government spending, while the latter involves a larger role for markets. Within my lifetime, there's been a preference shift from more government to less, but that doesn't mean inequality can't be reduced. It *can* be if the market itself distributes income more evenly.

In 1944, when I was two years old, my father, Leo Barnes, worked as an economist for the Office of Price Administration. (Other OPA employees included John Kenneth Galbraith and Richard Nixon.) As victory in World War II neared, many Americans feared another depression. With millions of soldiers returning and armament factories closing, a vast number of civilian jobs would be needed to keep everyone employed. What every American wanted to know was, where would all those new jobs come from?

My father offered a solution. In an article titled "The Economic Equivalent of War," he urged the creation of a peacetime government agency that would guarantee full employment by pledging, in advance, to buy up all the durable goods—cars, washing machines, and so on—that American factories produced but couldn't sell. As during the war, companies would be given production quotas by boards representing industry, labor, and the public; this would keep surpluses from getting out of hand. If surpluses got too high, the agency could order workweek reductions without pay cuts, thereby rewarding workers for greater productivity.[4] My father acknowledged that buying unsold hard goods would cost the Treasury several billion dollars a year but contended that such costs would be "incomparably smaller" than those of large-scale unemployment. "The proper shock absorber for economic dislocation in a democracy," he argued, "is the accumulation of inert commodities, not the living frustration of unemployment."

Rereading my father's proposal seventy years later, I must say that I like it a lot. It recognized that despite the harrowing scarcities of the 1930s, our modern economic machine has the ability to produce more stuff than we need with fewer workers than we have. In addressing this fundamental conundrum, my father's approach was broadly systemic. And, had it been adopted, it would have been good for businesses as well as workers.

That said, my father's proposal was also distinctly of its time. It relied on more government rather than less, and for that reason alone, it wouldn't fly today. Fortunately, the system changes we need today don't require larger government or higher taxes. What they do require is a more even flow of income within our economy. So the question we need to ask is, how can we create such a flow? What new pipes do we need, and what sort of income will flow through them?

———————

A FULLER ANSWER TO THESE QUESTIONS will occupy the rest of this book, but let's start by narrowing the possibilities.

First, we'll need new pipes to deliver income on a basis other than labor. These pipes should be capable of being installed in the not-too-distant future. This means they need to mesh with the pipes we have today.

Second, the new pipes should be solidly built. Anything that requires repeated refinancing by Congress isn't likely to last.

Third, the pipes should have — and be able to retain — a broad base of public support. This requires them to appeal across the political spectrum.

With these filters in mind, let's consider some possibilities. One is more progressive taxation than we now have — that is, raising taxes on the rich and flowing the added revenue into the US Treasury. Progressive taxes have been applied in varying degrees for a century or so, with generally positive results. But two things limit their effectiveness as a middle class prop: the power of the rich to evade taxes and the fact that, while progressive taxes may slightly reduce the wealth of the rich, they don't automatically lift the middle or the bottom.

Consider also a variation of my father's plan in which the government buys socially useful things such as bridge and highway improvements and clean energy systems, rather than surplus washing machines. Something like this was attempted in 2009 when, in the wake of financial collapse, President Obama persuaded Congress to enact an $825 billion "stimulus" package with spending on infrastructure, renewable energy, and education. A onetime grab bag of this sort, however, is a far cry from a permanent set of pipes. What's missing is a way to sustain the government's purchasing.

A more promising precedent is social insurance, a system for sharing the risks of unemployment, sickness, disability, and old-age poverty. Social insurance was invented in Germany in the 1880s and gradually installed in all industrial economies during the twentieth century. It's been more effective than progressive taxation in lifting the middle and lower classes, and it has the enormous virtue of automatic funding and distribution. It's a systemic solution to systemic problems that capitalism creates but doesn't solve. That is its genius and relevance here.

Equally interesting is that social insurance was the invention not of socialists but of the conservative chancellor Otto von Bismarck, who wanted to strengthen the German nation, build a prosperous economy, enlarge the middle class, and blunt the appeal of real socialists. Social insurance helped him do all these things at once.

Germany's system was a form of insurance because participants paid into a common fund and received benefits when needed. It was called *social* insurance because everyone was covered, and employers as well as the government chipped in.

Fast-forward to the United States in the 1930s. With unemployment at 25 percent, President Franklin Roosevelt's first task was to put millions of people to work. But another aspect of poverty required a different remedy. This poverty resulted not from financial collapse but from demographic changes that had begun decades earlier. America was no longer a rural society of multi-generational households; we'd become an urban, industrial nation of single-generation households. This meant that millions of aging parents were no longer cared for at home by their children. Moreover, because of improvements in public health and sanitation, people were living longer than ever. The result was that by 1939, more than three-quarters of Americans over sixty-five lived in poverty.[5]

Wisely, Roosevelt's advisers (especially Labor Secretary Frances Perkins) saw old-age poverty not as a temporary problem awaiting an upturn in economic activity, but as a systemic problem requiring a systemic solution. What emerged was the thirty-five-page Social Security Act, which, though brief in words, was monumental in impact.

The Social Security Act created a trust fund into which active workers and employers pay and out of which retired workers receive annuities — that is, monthly payments for life—much as Tom Paine proposed in 1797. The result is a self-financing, multigenerational system in which each generation supports its predecessors in return for being supported by its successors. The fund's trustees keep operating expenses low (they're currently 0.5 percent of the money handled),[6] and no private entity skims money off the top.

This simple system works so well that, once it was in place, future Congresses expanded it many times. They also added coverage for unemployment, workplace injuries, and medical care past age sixty-five. Today, social insurance amounts to 9 percent of our economy, and the poverty rate among elderly Americans is below 10 percent.[7]

Despite (or because of) social insurance's success, a portion of America's financial industry never liked it. These companies believed it was their right to protect Americans against risk and to be richly rewarded for doing so. So, not long after Social Security began, they mounted a nonstop campaign to privatize it.

One showdown came in 2005, when newly reelected President George W. Bush sought to create "personal accounts" out of a portion of Social Security contributions—accounts that would be managed by Wall Street. Much to Wall Street's surprise, however, there was so much opposition, even among Republicans, that the proposal never came to a vote. In the 2012 presidential election, Republican candidate Mitt Romney picked up the torch by calling for a voucher system to replace Medicare. This did not propel him to victory.

As it happened, Roosevelt anticipated opposition to social insurance and planned for it. When asked why Social Security was funded by payroll contributions rather than general taxes, he answered: "We put those payroll contributions there to give contributors a legal, moral, and political right to collect their pensions. That way, no damn politician can ever scrap Social Security."[8]

SOCIAL INSURANCE AS IT NOW STANDS can't solve the problems of the twenty-first century, but it offers several useful lessons.

Policies come and go; institutions endure. Social insurance is far more durable than tax laws or most other public policies. That's because it's not so much a policy as a set of self-financing institutions. As such, it's built into the fabric of people's lives. People make regular contributions and expect checks to arrive as promised. Undoing such institutions isn't easy.

Universality beats means testing. Virtually everyone in America is covered by social insurance; this gives it a huge middle-class constituency. It also makes social insurance very efficient: it serves more people for less money per capita than private insurance does or can, in part because it has no marketing or underwriting (deciding who is eligible) costs.

Universality also avoids the pejorative distinctions that come with means testing. If only economic "losers"

get benefits, they become "takers," "moochers," or whatever is the slur du jour. Those who don't get benefits
resent those who do, and those who do feel bad about
themselves. No one is happy with the arrangement.

Means testing, in short, divides society while universality unites it. To put it another way, means testing
necessarily pits one class against another—the very defi-
nition of class warfare—while universality treats us as a
single society.

Build external costs into current prices. Because of its contributory structure, roughly half the cost of supporting
workers in old age—the part that's covered by employer
contributions—is internalized into current prices. That's
because businesses include their social insurance contributions in their cost of goods sold. Other currently externalized costs ought to be treated the same way.

Build the pipes first; then add water. When Social Security
began, payroll contributions were 1 percent, benefits
were around $20 a month, and large categories of work-
ers were excluded. Over time, as the system became better known, it also became more popular. Benefits grew,
more people were covered, and health care was added.

President Roosevelt's Committee on Economic
Security, which drafted the original Social Security Act,
did so with this long-term vision in mind. "A program
of economic security, as we vision it, must have as its
primary aim the assurance of an adequate income to
each human being in childhood, youth, middle age, or

old age," the committee wrote in its report to Congress. "A piecemeal approach is dictated by practical considerations, but . . . whatever measures are deemed immediately expedient should be so designed that they can be embodied in the complete program."[9]

———/

THERE ARE TWO POTENTIAL ROUTES through which nonlabor income can flow: one runs through markets, the other through government. My preference is for the former. But as markets are constituted today, nonlabor income doesn't flow to nearly enough people. Some important pipes are missing.

The most obvious absence is a set of pipes that collect property income from multiple sources and spit it out to everyone. Such a system wouldn't be hard to build; it's essentially a mutual fund with some 300 million shareholders, each with a nontransferable share. It's safe to say that the software and hardware to run such a fund already exist. The barriers to building it are political, not technical.

In the remainder of the book I make the case for building such pipes, using as income sources wealth that already belongs, or should belong, to all of us equally. The governing principle behind these pipes would be *everyone-gets-a-share* rather than *winner-takes-all*. The new pipes wouldn't displace our existing ones—like social insurance, they'd complement them—but their equal distribution of a new sort of property income would offset the distorted distribution of the currently dominant sort. The result would be a market economy with a large and secure middle class, even as labor income declines.

To fully understand the case for adding these new pipes, it's necessary to understand how our existing ones work. This isn't always easy, but the basic patterns, if not the intricate details, can be discerned.

Our present pipes are designed to carry a mysterious substance I will henceforth call *rent*. Rent is mysterious because, despite its immensity, there's actually a "vast conspiracy" to keep it shrouded. (By "conspiracy" I mean here a loose network of billionaires, CEOs, lawyers, lobbyists, PR firms, politicians, and economists who benefit, first or second hand, from the current flow of rent.) The conspirators are keenly aware that the more hidden they can keep rent, the more of it they'll collect — and conversely, that the more broadly rent is noticed and understood, the more broadly it will be shared.

So let me tell you about rent, or more precisely, two kinds of rent: extracted and recycled. One is the dominant form today; the other is the kind we need more of tomorrow.

— 4 —

Extracted Rent

Forget about hard work and the merit system and honesty and all that crap, and get to where the Money River is.

—Kurt Vonnegut, *God Bless You, Mr. Rosewater*

When I cofounded Working Assets (now known as Credo) in 1983, we organized as a private corporation. Our corporate charter was our license to enter the American marketplace, with its 300 million consumers and all the legal, financial, and physical infrastructure Americans have built over generations. It also gave us the right to maximize financial gain for ourselves. We paid a pittance for these privileges and at no extra cost got limited liability and perpetual life. The entire package came with a timeless guarantee that our physical, intellectual, and financial property would be protected by the full authority of America's state and federal governments.

"Not a bad deal, starting a corporation," I mused at the time. "Sure, we may fail, and I may lose my investment, but if we win, we win big. And boy, is America behind us!"

Ten years later, when our annual sales passed $100 million, my partners and I realized that our closely held company would be worth millions more if we took it public. Thus, in addition to all the gifts America had already given us, we could pluck several extra million dollars out of thin air simply by floating a stock offering. Having just read Kurt Vonnegut's novel *God Bless You, Mr. Rosewater*, about a wealthy heir and the crafty lawyer who advises him, I thought I was getting close to the Money River.

In the end, the company's founders chose to remain closely held and forgo the "liquidity premium" we would have reaped had we sold our stock to strangers, figuring we were doing well enough, thank you, and would be happier (if poorer) outside the speculative vortex. I never regretted the choice. But that peek at the Money River piqued my interest.

Something had always mystified me about how fortunes are made in America. Clearly, the route to riches requires hard work and talent, but the magnitude of most fortunes wildly exceeds any reasonable compensation for either of these. Somewhere inside our economy lurks a magnifying machine that transforms legitimate rewards into grotesque riches. Hidden multipliers and takings are involved, and I wanted to locate them, if not profit from them. In other words, I wanted to find the Money River.

I had a few hunches where the river might lie. One came from my experience as a homeowner. If you bought a house for, say, $300,000 and sold it later for $400,000, you would pocket the difference. This is called a *capital gain*, and it would come not from anything you did, but because more people wanted to live in your neighborhood. That's a function of many things—population growth, schools, public transportation, and so on—that have nothing whatsoever to do with your labor or talent. They're societal phenomena or government provisions.

These societal gifts, moreover, are multiplied by financial leverage. You didn't actually pay $300,000 for the house when you bought it. You paid, say, $30,000 of your own money and borrowed the rest. Then, over the years, you paid down the mortgage to, say, $200,000. When you sold the house for $400,000, you paid off the mortgage and kept $200,000. So, for an initial investment of $30,000, you walked away with a net gain of $170,000. That's a 467 percent return for buying and selling a piece of property. A century ago, the American economist Thorstein Veblen called it "something for nothing."[1]

A similar sort of leverage kicks in when founders of a private company go public. This might be called *equity leverage* (as opposed to debt leverage), and its effect can be even more spectacular. Equity leverage works by incorporating anticipated future earnings into present asset prices, thereby enabling stock sellers to get a lump

sum now for a potential stream of future profits that may
or may not materialize. If a company is expected to grow,
this leverage can be huge—and it's on top of the liquidity premium that accrues simply from enlarging the universe of potential stock buyers. It's what enables people
like Mark Zuckerberg, founder of Facebook, to become
billionaires before they're thirty.

And that's not all. Large chunks of many fortunes
come from sources less visible than these. Consider
the nest egg of another youthful billionaire, Bill Gates.
According to *Forbes* magazine, Gates in 2013 was the
richest man in America and second-richest man in the
world, with a net worth of $72 billion.[2] Virtually all of
that comes from stock he received or bought cheaply as
Microsoft's cofounder. And from whence (besides equity
leverage and the liquidity premium) does the value of
that stock arise?

Here we move beyond multipliers into the realm of
takings. Microsoft wrote the code for its most profitable
products, the Windows operating system and the Office
applications, and marketed them ferociously. But it didn't
really invent them; it copied or adapted them from other
software. What's more, there's no lack of good alternatives
in the market. The reasons why people pay hundreds of
dollars, over and over, for unexceptional products that cost
just a few dollars to reproduce include the following:

- Everyone uses Microsoft programs, so if you want to
  be compatible, you have to use them, too.

- Your computer manufacturer preinstalled them and included them in the price of your computer.

- You can't borrow them from friends because they're copyrighted.

Thus, a sizable portion of Microsoft's stock value — arguably the lion's share — comes from system properties such as the network effect, market power, and copyright protection, a gift for which our government charges nothing. On top of this, Microsoft benefits from decades of public investment in schools, semiconductors, and the Internet; centuries of scientific progress; and unstinting generosity from nature (think of the fuels and atmosphere required to power the Internet). When you add it all up, you can't help but conclude that a large portion of Gates's fortune wasn't earned by him but rather was taken by him from wealth that rightfully belongs to everyone.

How much of what we call private wealth is taken in ways like these and systemically magnified rather than genuinely earned by its recipient? If you asked Warren Buffett, the second-richest American after Gates, he'd say, "A very significant percentage."[3] If you asked Nobel economist Herbert Simon, he'd be somewhat more precise. "If we're very generous with ourselves, I suppose we might claim we 'earned' as much as one-fifth of our income. The rest is patrimony associated with being a member of an enormously productive social system."[4]

The more one thinks about these things, the more one sees that behind all large fortunes lies a plethora of undeserved rewards. It is this that constitutes the Money River, and the highly limited access to it accounts for our highly skewed distribution of wealth.

———————

THE LONDON UNDERGROUND ABOUNDS with warnings to "mind the gap," referring to the space between station platforms and train doors. In our larger society, similar warnings could be issued about the gaps between rich and poor and between humans and nature. These gaps must be not only minded but also narrowed. The persistent question is how to do this, and I contend that *rent* is a useful and indeed necessary tool.

But before we get to that, we must first become familiar with rent. The term was first used by classical economists, including Adam Smith, to describe money paid to landowners. It was one of three income streams in the early years of capitalism, the others being wages paid to labor and interest paid to capital.

In Smith's view, landlords benefited from land's unique ability to enrich its owners "independent of any plan or project of their own."[5] This ability arises from the fact that the supply of good land is limited, while the demand for it steadily rises. The effect of landowners' collection of rent, he concluded, isn't to increase society's wealth, but to take money away from labor and capital.

Thus, land rent is an extractor of wealth rather than a contributor to it.

A century later, a widely read American economist named Henry George (his magnum opus, *Progress and Poverty*, sold over two million copies) enlarged Smith's insight substantially.[6] At a time when Karl Marx was blaming capitalists for expropriating surplus value from workers, George blamed landowners for expropriating rent from everyone. Such rent extraction operated like "an immense wedge being forced, not underneath society, but through society. Those who are above the point of separation are elevated, but those who are below are crushed down." George's proposed remedy was a steep tax on land that would recapture for society most of landowners' parasitic gains. But unlike Paine, who would have returned recaptured rent to everyone, George would have left it in government's hands.

In the twentieth century, the concept of rent was expanded to include monopoly profits, the extra income a company reaps by quashing competition and raising prices. Smith had previously written about this form of wealth extraction, but he didn't call it rent. "The interest of any particular branch of trade or manufactures is always to widen the market and to narrow the competition. . . . To widen the market may frequently be agreeable enough to the interest of the public; but to narrow the competition must always be against it, and can only serve to enable the dealers, by raising their profits above

Figure 4.1: ADAM SMITH'S "ABSURD TAX"

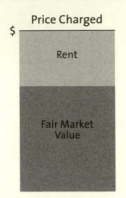

what they naturally would be, to levy, for their own benefit, an absurd tax upon the rest of their fellow-citizens."[7]

It's important to recognize that the tax Smith spoke of
isn't the kind we pay to government; it's the kind we pay,
much less visibly, to businesses. That's because prices in
capitalism are driven by four factors: supply, demand,
market power, and political power. The first two determine what might be called *fair market value*; the last two
determine what is now called rent. Actual prices charged
are the sum of fair market value and rent. Another way to
say this is that rent is the extra money people pay above
what they'd pay in truly competitive markets.

The contemporary concept of rent also includes income from privileges granted by government—import
quotas, mining rights, subsidies, tax loopholes, and so
on. Many economists use the term *rent seeking* to describe
the multiple ways in which special interests manipulate

government to enrich themselves at the expense of others. If you're wondering why Washington, DC, and its environs have grown so prosperous in recent decades, it's not because government itself has become gargantuan, it's because rent seeking has.

In short, rent is income received not because of anything a person or business produces but because of rights or power a person or business possesses. It consists of takings from the larger whole rather than additions to it. It redistributes wealth within an economy but doesn't add any. As British economist John Kay put it in the *Financial Times*, "When the appropriation of the wealth of others is illegal, it's called theft or fraud. When it's legal, it's called rent."[8]

BECAUSE RENT ISN'T LISTED SEPARATELY on any price tag or corporate income statement, we don't know exactly how much of it there is, but it's likely there's quite a lot. Consider, for example, health care in America, about one-sixth of our economy. There are many reasons why the United States spends 80 percent more per capita on health care than does Canada, while achieving no better results, but one of the biggest is that Canada has wrung huge amounts of rent out of its health-care system and we haven't.[9] Every Canadian is covered by nonprofit rather than profit-maximizing health insurance, and pharmaceutical prices are tightly controlled.

By contrast, in the United States, drug companies overcharge because of patents, Medicare is barred from bargaining for lower drug prices, and private insurers add many costs and inefficiencies.[10] Not even major reforms won by President Obama in 2010 are likely to change this. Indeed, by expanding coverage, they may actually *increase* the rent extracted by health-related companies.

Or consider our financial sector. Commercial banks, the kind that take deposits and make loans, receive an immensely valuable gift from the federal government: the right to create money. They're allowed to do this through what's called *fractional reserve banking*, which lets them lend, with interest, about ten times more than they have on deposit.[11] This gift alone is worth billions.

Then there are commercial banks' cousins, investment banks, which are in the business of trading securities. They can't mint money the way commercial banks do, but they have tricks of their own. For one, they charge hefty fees for taking private companies public, thus seizing part of the liquidity premium that public trading creates. For another, they make lofty sums by creating, and then manipulating, hyper-complex financial "products" that are, in effect, bets on bets. This pumps up the casino economy and extracts capital that could otherwise benefit the real economy.

For many decades, the Glass-Steagall Act of 1933 prevented a single company from being both a commercial and an investment bank. The law's reasoning was that since commercial banks are federally insured, they shouldn't engage in the riskier activities of investment banks. In the 1980s and '90s, however, banking regulations were trimmed, and New Deal laws, including Glass-Steagall, were repealed. By the time the housing bubble burst in 2008, financial companies were reaping about a third of all corporate profits, an astounding proportion that doesn't reflect the huge bonuses they paid their top employees (such bonuses *reduced* their profits by $18 billion in 2008).[12] Even more amazing, by 2010, less than two years after the biggest taxpayer-funded bailout in history, the banks' profits and bonuses were back to pre-crash levels.[13]

We could wander through other major industries — energy, telecommunications, broadcasting, agriculture — and find similar extractions of rent. What percentage of our economy, then, consists of rent? This is a question you'd think economists would explore, but few do. To my knowledge, the only prominent economist who has even raised it is Joseph Stiglitz, a Nobel laureate at Columbia University, and he hasn't answered it quantitatively.

The amount of rent in the US economy, Stiglitz says, is "hard to quantify [but] clearly enormous." Moreover, "to a significant degree," it "redistributes money from those at the bottom to those at the top." Further, it not only adds no value to the economy but "distorts resource allocation and makes the economy weaker."[14] And finally: "There's no begrudging the wealth accrued by those who have transformed our economy — the inventors of the computer, the pioneers of biotechnology. But, for the most part, these are not the people at the top of our economic pyramid. Rather, to a too large extent, it's people who have excelled at rent seeking in one form or another."

EIGHTY YEARS AGO, JOHN MAYNARD KEYNES looked forward to what he called "the euthanasia of the rentier." That day would come when the supply of capital was so large, relative to the demand for it, that the return to capital "would have to cover little more than [its] exhaustion by wastage and obsolescence together with some margin to cover risk and the exercise of skill and judgment." At that point, Keynes opined, "the intelligence and determination and executive skill of the financier will be harnessed to the service of the community on reasonable terms of reward."[15]

Alas, it was not to be. In seeming defiance of the laws of supply and demand, the rentier class, rather than disappearing, has ascended to new heights. How this happened is a long story, the essence of which is that, with the help of a compliant political class, the captains of finance built an enormous casino in which, thanks to leverage and legerdemain, unnaturally high returns can still be won.

A modest poker parlor for the rich would be one thing, but the magnitude of this floating casino is staggering. Consider these numbers:

- The global value of financial derivatives in 2012 was $687 trillion.[16] That compares to a total world GDP of $72 trillion.

- The total value of foreign exchange transactions in 2010 was $1.5 quadrillion (a quadrillion is 1,000 trillion). Of that amount, only 1.5 percent was used to pay for real goods. The rest was currency speculation.[17]

I focus on this bloated casino because it's both a problem and an opportunity. The problem is that it extracts billions from our real economy and leads to bubbles, crashes, and extreme inequality. The opportunity—if we seize it—lies in the possibility to redirect some of these extractions to real people and businesses.

Recycled Rent

You built a factory and it turned into something terrific — God bless!
Keep a hunk of it. But part of the underlying social contract is
you take a hunk of that and pay forward
for the next kid who comes along.

— Senator Elizabeth Warren

So far, I've described rent as a negative force in our economy. Now I want to present it as a potentially positive force — as money that, rather than being extracted by a few, is shared among many. I'll call this virtuous variant *recycled rent*.

There are two key differences between extracted and recycled rent. The first has to do with how the rent is collected, the second with how it's distributed.

The collection of extracted rent is done by businesses whose market and/or political power enables them to charge higher-than-competitive prices. It leads to unnecessarily high costs that serve no economic, social, or ecological purpose. Recycled rent, by contrast, is money that we, as co-owners, receive from businesses that use our co-owned assets. It too can lead to higher prices but for good reasons: to make businesses pay costs they currently shift to society, nature, and future generations, and to counterbalance extracted rent.

The second difference is distributional. Extracted rent flows upward to the small minority that owns most of the stock of rent-extracting businesses. Recycled rent, by contrast, flows to everyone equally.

At the moment, of course, extracted rent totals trillions of dollars a year, while recycled rent (outside of Alaska) is a concept rather than a reality. But the core idea of this book is that recycled rent can and should grow.

To understand how recycled rent could grow, it's necessary to explore two other concepts: co-owned wealth and externalities.

Co-owned wealth has several components. One consists of gifts of nature we inherit together: our atmosphere and watersheds, forests and fertile plains, and so on. In almost all cases, we overuse these gifts because there's little or no cost attached to doing so.

Another chunk of co-owned wealth is gifted to us by our ancestors: sciences and technologies, legal and political systems, our financial infrastructure, and much more. These confer enormous benefits on all of us, but a small minority reaps far more from them than does the large majority.

Yet another trove of co-owned wealth is what might be called "wealth of the whole"—the value added by the scale and synergies of our economy itself. The notion of "wealth of the whole" dates back to Adam Smith's insight two-and-a-half centuries ago that labor specialization and the exchange of goods—pervasive features of a whole system—are what make nations rich. Beyond that, it's obvious that no business can prosper by itself: all businesses need customers, suppliers, distributors, highways, money, and a web of complementary products (cars need fuel, software needs hardware, and so forth). So not only is our economy as a whole greater than the sum of its many parts; it's also a highly valuable asset itself, without which its parts would have almost no value at all.

The sum of wealth created by nature, our ancestors, and our economy as a whole is what I here call *co-owned wealth*. Some, including myself, have called it *shared wealth*, *the commons*, or *common wealth*.[1] Whatever we call it, it's the goose that lays almost all the eggs of private wealth.

Several things can be said about co-owned wealth. First, because it's not created by any individual or business, it belongs to all of us jointly. Second, because no one has a greater claim to it than anyone else, it belongs to all of us equally, or as close to equally as we can arrange.

A third thing that can be said about co-owned wealth is that we're managing it terribly. Several years ago, Jonathan Rowe, David Bollier, and I decided to audit America's co-owned wealth and report back to its owners, much as corporations report to theirs. We surveyed a broad sample of shared assets and found that "maintenance is terrible, theft is rampant, and rents often aren't being collected." To correct these persistent problems, we recommended sweeping management changes — not just new people dropped into old slots but new institutions designed to manage co-owned wealth responsibly.[2]

The big, rarely asked question about our current economy is *who gets the benefits of co-owned wealth*? No one disputes that private wealth creators are entitled to the wealth they create, but who is entitled to the wealth we share is an entirely different question. My contention is that the rich are rich not so much because they create wealth but because they capture a much larger share of co-owned wealth than they're entitled to. Another way to say this is that the rich are as rich as they are — and the rest of us are poorer than we should be — because extracted rent far exceeds recycled rent. That being so, the remedy is to diminish the first kind of rent and increase the second.

———————

EXTERNALITIES ARE THE COSTS that businesses impose on
others — workers, communities, nature, and future generations — but don't pay themselves. The classic example
is pollution.

Almost all economists accept the need to "internalize
externalities," by which they mean making businesses
pay the full costs of their activities. What they don't often discuss are the new income streams that would arise
if businesses actually did this. If they did, they'd have to
confront the question of whom businesses should pay
when they internalize their externalized costs.

This isn't a trivial question. In fact, it's among the most
momentous questions we must address in the twenty-
first century. The sums involved can, and indeed *should*,
be very large — after all, to diminish harms to nature and
society, we must internalize as many unpaid costs as possible. But whose money is it?

One answer was proposed nearly a century ago by
British economist Arthur Pigou, a colleague of Keynes's
at Cambridge. When the price of a piece of nature is too
low, Pigou said, government should impose a tax on it.
Such a tax would reduce our usage while raising revenue
for government. In this model, businesses would internalize their externalities by writing checks to government.

In theory, Pigou's idea makes sense; the trouble with
it lies in implementation. No western government wants
to get into the business (at least in peacetime) of price set-

ting; that's a job best left to markets. And even if politicians *tried* to adjust prices with taxes, there's little chance they'd get them "right" from nature's perspective. Far more likely would be tax rates driven by the very corporations that dominate government and overuse nature now.

An alternative would be to bring some nongovernmental entities into play; after all, the reason we have externalities in the first place is that no one represents stakeholders harmed by shifted costs. But if those stakeholders *were* represented by legally accountable agents, that problem could be fixed. The void into which externalities now flow would be filled by trustees of co-owned wealth. And those trustees would charge rent.

As for whose money it is, it follows from the above that payments for most externalities—and in particular, for costs imposed on nature and future generations—should flow to all of us together as the rightful co-owners of shared wealth. They certainly shouldn't flow to the companies that impose the externalities; that would defeat the purpose of internalizing them. But neither should they flow to government, as Pigou and others have suggested.

In my mind, there's nothing wrong with government *taxing* our individual shares of co-owned wealth rent, just as it taxes other personal income, but government shouldn't get first dibs on it. The proper first claimants are we, the people. One could even argue, as economist Dallas Burtraw has, that government capture of this income may be an unconstitutional taking of private property.[3]

THIS BRINGS US BACK TO RECYCLED RENT. In essence, recycled rent is rent charged for use of co-owned wealth
that's paid to its rightful owners (see figure 5.1). Several
points can be made about this sort of rent.

First, paying rent to ourselves would have a very different effect than paying rent to Wall Street, Bill Gates,
or Saudi princes. In addition to discouraging overuse
of nature, it would return the money we paid in higher
prices to where it did our families and economy the most
good: our own pockets. From there we could spend it on
food, housing, or anything else we chose. Such spending
would not only help *us*; it would also help businesses and
their employees. It would be like a bottom-up stimulus
machine in which people rather than government do the
spending. This would be no small virtue at a time when
fiscal and monetary policies have lost their potency.

Figure 5.1: RECYCLED RENT

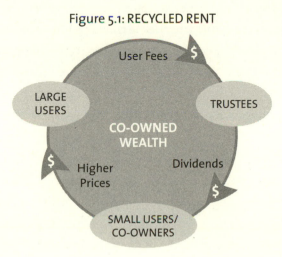

Second, recycled rent isn't a set of policies that can be changed when political winds shift. Rather, it's a set of pipes that, once in place, would circulate money indefinitely, thereby sustaining a large middle class and a healthier planet even as governments came and went.

And third, though recycled rent requires government action to get started, it has the political virtue of avoiding the bigger/smaller government tug-of-war that paralyzes Washington today. It is, after all, property income that doesn't enlarge government. It could therefore appeal to, or at least not offend, voters and politicians in the center, left, and right.

A TRIM TAB IS A TINY FLAP ON A SHIP or airplane's rudder. The designer Buckminster Fuller often noted that moving a trim tab slightly turns a ship or a plane dramatically. If we think of our economy as a moving vessel, the same metaphor can be applied to rent. Depending on how much of it is collected and whether it flows to a few or to many, rent can steer an economy toward extreme inequality or a large middle class. It can also guide an economy toward excessive use of nature or a safe level of use. In short, in addition to being a wedge (as Henry George put it), rent can be a rudder. And our economy's outcomes can dramatically shift depending on how we turn it.

Think about the board game Monopoly. The object is to squeeze so much rent out of other players that you wind up with all their money. You do this by acquiring monopolies and building hotels on them. However,

there's another feature of the game that offsets this extracting of rent: all players get a cash payment when
they pass Go. (In my day, the payment was $200; nowa-
days it's $200,000.) This can be thought of as recycled
rent.

As Monopoly is designed, the rent extracted through
monopoly power greatly exceeds the rent returned to
players when they pass Go. The result is that the game
always ends the same way: one player gets all the money.
But suppose we built a wider set of pipes for recycled
rent, then decreased the amount of extracted rent and
increased the flow of the recycled kind. For example, we
might pay $1,000 for passing Go and reduce hotel rents
by half. What would happen then?

Instead of flowing upward and concentrating in the
hands of a single winner, rent would flow more evenly.
Instead of the game ending when one winner takes all,
the game would continue with many players remaining.
An everyone-gets-a-share flow of rent might not be as
exciting as a winner-take-all flow, but it would wreak
less havoc, benefit more players, and last longer.

The point I wish to make is that different rent flows
can steer a game—and, more important, an economy—
toward different outcomes. Among the outcomes that
can be altered are levels of wealth concentration, pollution, and real business investment as opposed to specula-
tion. Rent is thus a powerful tool. And it's also something
we can fiddle with. Do we want less extracted and more
recycled rent? If so, we can build the requisite pipes and
start filling them.

The Alaska Model

Our dividend program simply gives back to the people a portion of earnings from invested oil wealth that belongs to the people.

—Former governor Jay Hammond

Jay Hammond, the Republican governor of Alaska from 1974 to 1982 and father of the Alaska Permanent Fund, led a life nearly as exciting as Thomas Paine's. He was a Marine fighter pilot during World War II, then a bush pilot, commercial fisherman, and backcountry guide in Alaska. Friends urged him to run for local office, then the state legislature, and then for governor, all of which he did with some reluctance. After retiring as governor, he moved with his native wife to a remote lakeside cabin accessible only by float plane. He died in 2005, a state hero.

It's unlikely that Hammond read, *Agrarian Justice*. Nevertheless, he conceived and then persuaded legislators and voters in a ruggedly individualist state to adopt the world's first universal dividend-paying fund of the sort that Paine envisioned. He did this, and the people of Alaska approved it, not out of any ideology but because it just made sense.

As Hammond told the story, the Alaska Permanent Fund began with fish. In the early 1960s, Hammond was living in Naknek, a ramshackle village on the shore of Bristol Bay, one of the richest fisheries in the world. He couldn't help noticing that although the villagers were dirt poor, out-of-state companies were extracting billions of dollars' worth of fish every year. While serving as mayor of Bristol Bay Borough (population 1,147 in 1970), Hammond proposed levying a 3 percent tax on fish and putting the proceeds into an investment fund that would pay dividends to all local residents. He called the plan "Bristol Bay, Inc.," but it was rejected by skeptical voters.[1]

After his election as governor, Hammond floated a similar proposal, which he called "Alaska, Inc." Revenue would come from an extraction tax on natural gas, and dividends would be paid as credits against state income taxes. This time his proposal passed the legislature. Millions of new dollars flowed into state coffers, and a small portion of that went back to Alaskans as tax credits.

Governor Jay Hammond of Alaska, in 1976.

(Courtesy Alaska State Library, P213-4-009)

Hammond wrote soon afterward that "almost no one remembered the tax credits. At that point I decided that if another dividend program was established, I wanted to put a check in everyone's hand. I thought that by doing so people would better appreciate the dividend and demand that the state maximize returns from its resource wealth."[2]

As fate would have it, Hammond had one more chance to launch a dividend program. This time the revenue source was potentially huge: royalties from the state-owned North Slope oil field. "I wanted to transform oil wells pumping oil for a finite period into money wells pumping money for infinity," he explained. The way to do that was to put a large chunk of the royalties into a joint savings account that would benefit not only today's Alaskans but also tomorrow's. The saved money would be invested and grow over time. Paying out some of the earnings in dividends would assure that politicians wouldn't squander the rest of it. After much hemming and hawing, the legislature passed a version of Hammond's plan. Voters then approved it in a referendum by two to one.

At this point, the US Supreme Court stepped in. The original formula for distributing dividends wasn't one person, one share; it was one share for each year an adult had lived in Alaska since 1959, the year Alaska became a state. Hammond's thinking was that physical residence was a form of "investment" in the state that should be rewarded with financial equity.

For obvious reasons, the formula was popular with old-timers but not with newcomers. Two of the latter, who happened to be lawyers, sued the state for violating their right to equal protection under the Fourteenth Amendment. The Supreme Court, with only one dissent, supported the plaintiffs, in effect making Paine's formula—one person, one share—the default formula for distributing natural wealth within a state.[3] A state could choose an unequal formula, the court allowed, if the formula "rationally furthers a legitimate state purpose," but it couldn't "divide citizens into . . . permanent classes."

In response to the high court's ruling, the legislature changed the dividend formula to one person, one share, and extended eligibility to all Alaskans, including children, who had resided in the state for six months or more. (In 1990, it changed the residency requirement to one year.) Hammond later acknowledged that the per capita formula "accorded the Permanent Fund even greater protection by expanding its benefits to a far greater number of Alaskans."[4]

Since 1980, the fund has grown from $900 million in assets to over $44 billion, thanks to both its oil income and its conservative approach to investing. It has paid yearly dividends to all Alaskans that have regularly topped $1,000 ($4,000 for families of four) and peaked at $3,269 per person in 2008 (see figure 6.1 on page 76). And it has withstood attempts by the legislature to "invade" it for public spending or tax reduction. In short, it has fulfilled Hammond's vision of sharing and preserving the financial value of Alaska's natural gifts.

THE ALASKA PERMANENT FUND has been around long enough to yield lessons not just about the fund itself but more broadly about dividends from co-owned wealth. These include the following:

A universal dividend system works —at all levels. Operationally, it's easy and inexpensive to administer; the Permanent Fund's expenses are less than 0.3 percent of its assets.[5] The dividends, which were initially paid by check and mailed, are now wired to people's bank accounts at a cost of pennies per transaction. Enrollment is also done online. There are no incomes to verify and virtually no fraud to prosecute.

Economically, the dividends have kept oil money within the state and stimulated Alaska's economy from the bottom up. They've also reduced poverty and made Alaska one of the least unequal states in America.[6]

Politically, the Permanent Fund remains one of the most popular government initiatives ever. Politicians in both parties sing its praises. The chances for repeal, or even reduction, are essentially nil. One attempt in 1999 to transfer money from the Permanent Fund to the state treasury was trounced in a referendum by 83 percent of voters.

A dividend-paying fund can protect future generations by benefiting the living. It's extremely difficult to get today's citizens to act on behalf of tomorrow's. One of the great virtues of the Permanent Fund is that it aligns the interests of current and future generations. By paying dividends today, it assures that there'll be co-owned wealth tomorrow.

In Alaska's case, natural wealth today is turned into nonlabor income for all residents today and tomorrow. But that's not the only possible intergenerational deal. For example, as we'll soon see, natural wealth today can be *maintained* as natural wealth tomorrow by generating nonlabor income today.

It's also the case that neither the Permanent Fund, nor any fund based on co-owned wealth, imposes a financial burden on future generations. Such funds make no commitment to pay predefined benefits; they pay out only what's earned in a given year. In political speak, they're about as fiscally responsible as you can get. In econospeak, they create no unfunded liabilities or any possibility of adding to government debt.

Offshoots happen. Once a dividend system is in place, it can add features and revenue with relative ease. The simplest add-ons are options to earmark dividends. Today, Alaskans can automatically assign part or all of their dividends to tax-sheltered college savings accounts or tax-deductible charities. On top of this, additions to the Permanent Fund have been made from time to time by the legislature. These have increased the assets in the Fund and thus the size of future dividends.

The most spectacular addition occurred in 2008 at the behest of Republican governor Sarah Palin. The year was characterized by soaring gasoline prices and unprecedented oil company profits. Palin responded by slapping an excess profits tax on the state's oil companies and using the revenue to boost that year's dividend by $1,200. When queried about this by Sean Hannity on Fox News, Palin replied, "What we're doing up there is returning a share of resource development dollars back to the people who own the resources. Our constitution mandates that as you develop resources, it's to be for the maximum benefit of the people, not the corporations, not the government, but the people of Alaska."[7]

For sustaining a large middle class, dividends are better than tax credits. There are tax credits for parents of college students, buyers of electric cars, investors in oil and gas, beekeepers, certain types of research, low-income housing, and other politically favored activities. Politicians love to dispense funds this way because they don't appear as expenditures and are usually unnoticed by those

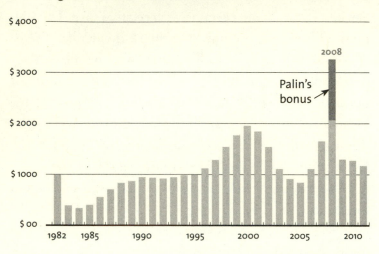

Figure 6.1: ALASKA PERMANENT FUND DIVIDENDS

who pay for them (all taxpayers who don't get the tax credits). However, as a way to compensate the general public, tax credits don't have the same resonance as dividends do—as Hammond recognized.

The reason is pretty obvious yet not widely grasped by the political class. To economists and often to politicians, a dollar received in one form is identical to a dollar received in another; money, after all, is fungible. However, in the real world, the *way* money is delivered matters a lot. A tax credit is delivered in the form of lower withholding from a paycheck or less money owed on April 15. Neither form of delivery is likely to be perceived by an untrained eye. And even if it is, the dominant reaction isn't likely to be gratitude for paying less tax but displeasure for paying what's still owed. A dividend, by contrast, arrives in both your bank account and

your brain without an accompanying tax bill. You can
see it, withdraw it at an ATM, include it in your budget, and spend it on anything you want. And if it's taken
away, you'll notice.

President Obama might have thought about this
in 2012. After campaigning for middle-class tax relief,
he was able to win approval for a payroll tax credit
that showed up as lower withholding from paychecks.
The credit was worth about $1,000 a year to an aver-
age family. Yet it disappeared with nary a squeal when
Republicans demanded cuts in the federal deficit. Had
the money been delivered as dividends, it would in all
likelihood still be flowing.

Dividends—especially if they come from co-owned
wealth—have another perceptual advantage. According
to several surveys, most Alaskans view their dividends
not as government handouts but as their rightful share
of the state's natural wealth.[8] Thus, there's no stigma attached to receiving them. Further, any attempt by politicians to reduce the dividends is seen as an encroachment
on legitimate property rights.

Dividends for All

The spectrum is just as much a national resource as our national forests. That means it belongs to every American equally.

—Former Senator Bob Dole

What Alaska has done with oil, our whole country can do with air, money, and other co-owned assets. But before I show how, it's worth exploring other ways to spread nonlabor income broadly.

A citizen's income. A basic income guarantee, or citizen's income, is an equal amount paid by government to all, with the money coming from general taxes. There's no means test and the income is unconditional. Leading advocates have included economists Robert Theobald and Nobel Prize winner James Tobin.[1] In 1968, Paul Samuelson, John Kenneth Galbraith, and 1,200 other economists signed a document supporting the idea.[2] Four years later, a modest version ($1,000 per person per year) was proposed by presidential candidate George McGovern, whom Tobin advised. Called a "demogrant," it was poorly explained, badly received, and quickly withdrawn. No major US politician has proposed anything like it again, though the idea has caught on in Europe (see chapter 9).

A guaranteed minimum income. This approach is similar to the citizen's income, in that funding would come from general taxes, but different in that would not be universal: it would go only to people who need it and cover only what they need to reach the minimum. Milton Friedman's "negative income tax," first proposed in 1962, is the most prominent version of this model.[3]

Friedman's idea was that people whose yearly earnings fell below a politically set line would receive a tax "refund" equal to the difference. The refund would be paid even if the recipient owed no taxes. The advantage of using the tax system to top off low incomes, he argued, was that it had a built-in means test and cash distribution system.

The closest Congress ever came to adopting a form of negative income tax was in 1970 when, after years of riots in American cities, President Richard Nixon proposed his so-called Family Assistance Plan. The plan was intended to help, or at least quiet, the urban poor by guaranteeing every family of four a minimum of $1,600 a year. To appease liberals, who thought $1,600 was a paltry sum, Nixon added a 50 percent federal subsidy to states that increased the minimum above $1,600. To attract conservatives, he included a requirement that able-bodied men—though not single mothers—be willing to accept "suitable work," which if they did would reduce their family assistance. Nixon's bill passed the House but died in the Senate. Interestingly, Friedman lobbied against it because it didn't eliminate welfare.

A scaled-back version of the negative income tax is the Earned Income Tax Credit, or EITC, which focuses on low-paid workers. First created in 1975 with bipartisan support, it has been increased over the years to a maximum of $5,750 for a family of five. In 2010, about 27 million low-income households received some benefit from the EITC, but few got the maximum because as recipients earn more by working, the tax refund phases out.[4] And students, the unemployed, and retired people get nothing.

Universal stock ownership. One of the most original economic thinkers of the last century, Louis Kelso, took a different approach to spreading nonlabor income. Kelso was a San Francisco lawyer and investment banker who is best known for inventing employee stock ownership plans, or ESOPs, which now cover about ten million Americans.[5] He's less known for his deeper analysis of modern capitalism that sheds considerable light on the plight of our middle class.

In modern times, Kelso argued, most of the gains in economic productivity come not from labor but from new technologies and systems. Since capital owners benefit far more from technology and systems than workers do, capitalism as we know it increasingly shifts income to capital owners. A democratic and still capitalist remedy is to give increasingly more people access to corporate stock. Employee stock ownership plans are a step in this direction, and Kelso's breakthrough was to create a way to finance them (through trusts that buy stock on credit) and get them favorable tax treatment.

ESOPs, however, have two limitations: they're limited to workers in companies that choose to adopt them, and they suffer from the fact that putting all one's eggs in a single company's stock isn't as safe as putting them in a diversified portfolio. A larger leap toward broad stock ownership would be a plan that covered everyone and included stock in a broad assortment of companies.[6]

Just such a plan was proposed in 2007 by Dwight Murphey, a follower of free-market economist Ludwig von Mises. Unlike many conservatives, who blame the poor themselves and government programs for poverty, Murphey acknowledges that most modern poverty is due to a lack of jobs that pay well. Murphey also recognizes that the shortage of good-paying jobs now affects the middle class as well as the poor. Given these realities, and given his preference for minimal government, Murphey proposed a "shared market economy" in which everyone receives income from corporate stock.[7]

At the core of his model is a family of mutual funds, governed in a way that would assure their independence from politics. These mutual funds would invest in a broad cross-section of companies. Over time, they'd accumulate substantial holdings and, like the Alaska Permanent Fund, pay dividends from their earnings. The capital to acquire the holdings would come from the US Treasury, which would borrow it from the Federal Reserve.

The mutual funds themselves would be owned by all Americans, one person, one share. The result, Murphey argues, would be "a broad distribution of the ownership of competitive capitalism, providing incomes and purchasing power to all, while at the same time furnishing business firms with abundant capital."[8]

IN THINKING ABOUT THESE MODELS, it's easy to get lost in the details. What concerns me here, though, aren't the specifics of each model but the philosophical and political choices that lie beneath them. Of these, the most important are whether eligibility should be universal or based on need, and where the money should come from.

The answer to the first question depends on the goal being sought. If the goal is to reduce poverty, a good case can be made for basing eligibility on need. On the other hand, if the goal is to sustain a large middle class, the case for universality is much stronger.

Need-based distribution necessarily divides society into two camps, higher-income payers and lower-income recipients. The former resent that money is taken from them, while the latter resent being viewed as welfare recipients.

Need-based distribution also creates a work disincentive that the middle class won't appreciate any more than the poor. In all means-tested programs, the amount recipients receive necessarily declines as their earnings increase. Suppose that for every $2 you earn by working, you lose 50 cents in nonlabor income. That's hardly an incentive to work.

Universality, by contrast, unites society by putting all its members in the same boat. The income everyone receives is a birthright, not a handout. There's no means test and no penalty for working. This changes the story, the psychology, and the politics. No one is demonized, and a broad constituency protects the system from political attack.

The chief argument against universality is that it's wasteful. Why give Bill Gates money he clearly doesn't need? The reason is that if the aim is to sustain a broad middle class, excluding the richest few percent saves only a small amount of money at the cost of broad political support. Better to include everyone and tax the income at each recipient's marginal rate.

As for the second question—where the money should come from—the options are individual and employer contributions, taxes, and co-owned wealth. Individual and employer contributions are appropriate for retirement and insurance plans, such as Social Security and Medicare, but not as supplements to labor income; indeed, they're most often taken *from* labor income. That leaves taxes and co-owned wealth.

———————

THE CASE FOR TAXES IS MILTON FRIEDMAN'S: we have a tax system in place, so why not use it? The answer is that the four-million-word tax code is a permanent political war zone. Lobbyists whittle at it every day; nothing is fixed, everything is up for grabs. Moreover, any money that comes in through taxes is likely to be used by government for one program or another, or to reduce the federal debt, rather than to pay dividends to citizens.

Co-owned wealth provides a different playing field. The typical income source isn't a tax but a user fee, and it's collected not by the IRS but by an entity representing co-owners equally. This means the revenue bypasses government coffers and all the battles that surround them. It also means that the income can be dedicated to dividends, just as social insurance contributions are dedicated to benefits.

It's sometimes said that user fees are just a euphemism for taxes. If the revenue goes to government, that case can certainly be made. But if it goes to all of us as co-owners, it can't—for two reasons. First, whoever pays the user fee gets something of value in exchange. Whether it's permission to pollute our atmosphere or to benefit from our financial infrastructure, the user is paying for value received in a voluntary transaction. No coercion is involved.

Second, the fee is for the right to use another person's property, whether it's an ecosystem, an electromagnetic field, or a monetary system. Normally, when we use someone else's property, we pay them. This has nothing to do with government or taxes; it's how capitalism works. To *not* pay for using someone else's property is called trespassing.

In addition, dividends from co-owned wealth don't offend liberals or conservatives. They help the middle class and families with children in particular. They don't increase taxes or borrowing, expand government, or diminish liberty. So what's not to like?

It's no secret that Americans don't like redistributory schemes in which government taxes money people have already received and transfers it to other people. On the other hand, we love income from property. So why not derive dividends from wealth that's rightfully ours and eliminate a host of philosophical and political objections?

As evidence that shared ownership trumps taxes as a source of nonlabor income for all, consider the following exchange between Fox News commentators Bill O'Reilly and Lou Dobbs:

> O'REILLY: It's my contention that we the people own the gas and oil discovered in America. It's our land and the government administers it in our name. . . . Land and water are the domain of we the people.
>
> DOBBS: The oil that we're talking about belongs to us, as you said. . . . In Alaska, there's a perfect model for what we should do as a nation. We should have—let's

call it the American Trust. Have the oil companies put their fees into that trust, not to be touched by the Treasury Department or any other agency, but for investment on behalf of the American people. A couple of things then happen. One, it reminds everyone whose oil this is. And it even puts a little money, a little dollar sign, on what it's worth to be a citizen.[9]

———————

HOW MIGHT DIVIDENDS FROM CO-OWNED WEALTH work in practice? One possibility would be the following:

Imagine that whenever Americans get a Social Security number, they get two things along with it. One is the familiar retirement account; the other is a dividend account. Essentially, the latter represents a nontransferable share in a mutual fund that receives income from assets we co-own. Like a twenty-first century version of Paine's idea, the mutual fund would periodically wire dividends to its share-owners' personal bank accounts.

Why connect dividends to Social Security? One reason harks back to Milton Friedman: it has a distribution system already in place. That system is universal, efficient, and trusted. In over seventy-five years, it hasn't missed a payment. Its customer service is excellent, and Americans like it far more than the tax system.

A deeper reason is that shared wealth dividends enhance middle-class economic security and are a logical sequel to social insurance. While social insurance has eased many life risks, it hasn't achieved the fuller vision of Roosevelt's 1935 Commission, "an adequate income to each human being in childhood, youth, middle age, or old age." Fulfilling that larger vision requires revenue beyond individual and employer contributions, and that revenue could, and arguably should, flow from jointly owned wealth.

Like the existing Social Security revenue stream, the new one would be self-renewing and permanently dedicated—once in place, it would require no further congressional action to continue flowing. In other respects, the new revenue stream would differ from that of Social Security. First, it would add to, rather than subtract from, labor income. Second, it wouldn't encumber future generations; money paid out would never exceed money taken in. And third, it would require polluters to pay for their pollution and bankers to forgo some unearned profits, ancillary benefits that Social Security doesn't produce.

Co-owned wealth dividends would have one further benefit: they'd keep our economy humming by maintaining consumer purchasing power. Most economists agree that what drives economic activity is *aggregate demand*, a fancy term for consumer buying power. Our vast productive machine can churn out an endless quantity of goods, but if people can't pay for them, there's no point in making them. Businesses that do so will go broke.

Economists differ on how best to sustain aggregate demand—my father thought government should buy unsold durable goods—but virtually all agree that money spent right away stimulates economic activity better than money siphoned into speculative betting. That's because spent money has a multiplier effect. As Robert Reich has put it, "High aggregate demand creates a virtuous cycle."[10] When consumers buy more, businesses sell more, invest more, hire more workers, and create even more demand for goods and services. This turns the wheels of commerce faster than does money in a speculative cloud. The latter leads to asset bubbles and subsequent crashes but does little to create consumption, production, or real wealth.

WE'RE LEFT WITH THE QUESTION of how to fill the co-owned wealth pot—what assets, and in what quantities, should we put in it? This is a question that has no right or final answer—selecting which co-owned assets should pay dividends will always be a work in progress. But we can draw some general guidelines.

First, the pot should include a variety of assets, high among which should be our sinks for industrial wastes, especially the atmosphere. This asset is discussed more fully in the next chapter. Other potential assets include our monetary infrastructure, electromagnetic spectrum, and intellectual-property protection system. Further discussion of the value of these assets may be found in the appendix.

The reason why our monetary system is on this list goes back to Article I of our Constitution, which assigns the power to create money to Congress. In practice, however, over 90 percent of the money circulating today is created by commercial banks, at considerable benefit to themselves. This can properly be described as a privatization of the "coin of the realm," which historically was issued by the sovereign. If the sovereign today is no longer a king, neither is it a consortium of private banks. It is, according to our Constitution, we the people, as represented by Congress. And in reality, we the people are the backers of our national currency. If banks—or at least big banks—fail, we pick up the pieces. So if anyone should get the benefits from issuing new US currency, it should be us.

How do private banks create official US dollars? They do it through a process called *fractional reserve banking*. If you deposit $1,000, the banking system uses your money as a reserve to lend about $10,000. To make loans beyond your deposit, a bank simply creates the money electronically. As long as it holds about 10 percent of its loans in reserve (in case depositors want to withdraw cash), the bank is in compliance with the law.

What's the problem with this? One is that almost all the money in our economy is owed back to banks with interest. This means our overall debt burden is considerably higher than it needs to be.

Another is that private banks are walking off with a lot of money that could otherwise flow to us. Instead of letting banks create money by lending it to us, the Treasury or Fed could wire equal dividends to us directly, without interest or principal repayment required. This wouldn't create any more money than banks now do; it would just create it in a different way.[11]

Think about the board game Monopoly. Cash is added to the game every time a player passes Go. Absent those infusions, there wouldn't be enough money to build houses and hotels, and no one would get rich. We take this feature of Monopoly for granted, but notice: the new money isn't lent by the bank to players and then repaid with interest. Rather, it's given to players directly, equally, and debt free. This helps everyone buy property, increases general prosperity, and prevents the bank from hogging wealth.

One oft-heard objection to debt-free money distribution is that the Treasury would print too much of it, thereby triggering inflation. Banks, after all, are limited to lending a multiple of the money in their vaults, whereas government has no such limit. This danger could be averted, however, by having an independent board such as the Fed decide the quantity of money to be created, based on a mandate to prevent inflation.

The idea of debt-free distribution of money isn't new. During the Civil War, President Abraham Lincoln, rather than borrowing from banks, paid Union soldiers with freshly minted "greenbacks." Beginning in the 1930s, a succession of eminent economists, including Irving Fisher and Henry Simons, proposed returning the money-creation function to government.[12] Milton Friedman memorably imagined government "helicopter dropping" new money into the economy.[13] Recently, Lord Adair Turner, Britain's former top bank regulator, made a similar proposal, and even Ben Bernanke, former chair of the Fed, floated the idea—not for the United States but for Japan.[14]

To be sure, the primary concern of these economists and regulators wasn't to pay dividends; it was to reduce the amount of debt and systemic risk in our economy. Their preferred method for dropping money into our economy was for the federal government to print and spend it. But that's not the only way to do it. With Social Security's database and a few computers, it's just a hop-step from having the government spend new money to having the people spend it instead.

Directly issuing new money isn't the only way to generate revenue from our co-owned monetary infrastructure. There are also securities and currency trading systems we create, regulate, and rescue when they threaten to collapse. These trading systems are the casinos from which investment banks and hedge funds extract so much rent. If we were running a casino in Las Vegas, we'd take several percent off the top. But we charge Wall Street virtually nothing.

We could change that in several ways, however. The simplest would be to charge a small fee—half a percent or less—on trades of assets held for less than a year. This would encourage long-term investing as opposed to short-term betting. And the income from these fees could be added to the fund from which dividends are paid.

AS TO THE TOTAL QUANTITY OF ASSETS to put into the co-
owned wealth fund, my suggestion is: keep adding until
society decides the pot is full. Like social insurance, co-
owned wealth dividends will grow by laying pipes first
and then filling them with water. The long-term goal is
to pay dividends that modestly supplement labor income
for everyone. *When* that goal is reached is for the people,
through politics, to decide.

Still, it's worth estimating the quantity of money that
could flow through shared wealth dividends if the will
were there. For the next several decades, a sizable chunk
could come from selling a declining number of carbon
pollution permits. In addition, revenue could flow from
our monetary infrastructure and other shared resources.
Figure 7.1 lists five potential sources, along with estimates of their possible yields. It shows that a mature system could generate close to $5,000 per person per year,
or $20,000 a year for a family of four. The numbers are
explained in the appendix.

Consider what $5,000 per person per year would
mean. If a child's dividends were saved and invested
starting from birth, they'd yield enough to pay for a debt-
free college education at a public university. In midlife,
$5,000 per person would add 25 percent to the income
of a family of four earning $80,000 a year. In late life, it
would boost the average retiree's Social Security benefit
by about 30 percent.

Figure 7.1: POTENTIAL SOURCES OF DIVIDENDS
(in billions of 2013 dollars)

Shared Asset	Low	High	Middle
Atmospheric carbon storage	$87	$309	$198
Securities transaction fees	$268	$446	$357
New money creation	$244	$323	$284
Intellectual-property protection	$324	$324	$324
Spectrum use	$84	$84	$84
TOTAL	**$1,007**	**$1,486**	**$1,247**
Per capita share	$3,357	$4,953	$4,157
Family of four share	$13,428	$19,812	$16,628

AN OFT-CITED RISK OF PAYING PEOPLE money they don't work for is that they'll get lazy. This is the scare story that's thrown at every suggested method of reducing inequality, so it's wise to be skeptical. Has this happened to Alaskans, now exposed to twenty-five years of dividends? Sarah Palin wouldn't say so. And neither would any economic study.

Besides lacking empirical support, the road-to-laziness argument lacks logic. Why does it apply only to those at the bottom and middle of the income scale and not to those at the top, where immunity to the perils of nonlabor income happily reigns? One could argue that the rich have more "moral fiber" than the poor, but that would be difficult to prove. A more logical thesis, if one accepts the premise that the need for money motivates people to work, is that those at the bottom will always work at least as hard as those at the top.

The flip side of this argument is that even if some people did work less because of dividends, it might not be such a bad thing. Americans are among the most overworked people on the planet. According to the Organization for Economic Cooperation and Development, Americans in 2012 labored about ten weeks more per year than the Dutch and Germans, three weeks more than the British, and two weeks more than the Canadians.[15] We also have less vacation, sick leave, and family leave than workers in most other affluent nations. If dividends eased the pressure to work, we would likely be less stressed and healthier than we are now. And wages might even go up if employers really need us.

If Americans work fewer paid hours in the future, the chief reason won't be because we get dividends. It will be because technology and our economic system produce more wealth per hour of labor than they do today. And if that happens, we should celebrate *and* raise our dividends. We'll have more time to devote to family, friends, communities, and other interests. An ever-larger number of us will be able not only to pursue happiness but to enjoy it.

Carbon Capping:
A Cautionary Tale

Our planet's atmosphere is a sacred public trust that belongs to all of us, and the right to pollute it should not be given away for free.

—Senator Edward Markey

Many of the ideas discussed so far in theoretical terms collided with reality in 2009, when Congress attempted to limit carbon pollution in the United States. Like two previous attempts, this one failed. At the same time, though less noticed, Congress also missed an opportunity to create a fund that pays dividends to all Americans. The revenue for this fund would have come from selling rights to dump carbon dioxide into our co-owned air.

The story of these failures is both political and intellectual. In this chapter, I trace the transformation of a good idea — a market-based limit on carbon pollution — into a compromised and beaten one. This transformation was driven by the familiar Washington process of rent seeking, and its story yields a number of lessons.

THE IDEA OF CAPPING FLOWS of harmful substances, and then letting markets allocate them, goes back to 1968, when a Canadian economist, the late John Dales, floated the idea in a book called *Pollution, Property & Prices*.[1] At the time, Dales wasn't thinking about climate change; he was thinking about farmers who polluted streams with chemical runoffs. Some farmers could reduce their pollution more efficiently than others. If a declining quantity of pollution rights were issued and farmers could trade them, Dales argued, farmers themselves would find the cheapest ways to cut their pollution.

Economists, if not farmers, picked up the idea and started applying it, conceptually, to other forms of pollution. In doing this, they were influenced not just by Dales but also by Nobel Prize–winning economist Ronald Coase, who in an oft-quoted paper, "The Problem of Social Cost," argued that property rights could solve the problem of externalities without government regulation.[2] (Coase was part of the University of Chicago school of thought, which holds that markets do almost everything better than government.)

In 1990, the idea made its way into national legislation. That year's amendments to the Clean Air Act created a cap-and-trade system to reduce sulfur dioxide emissions from coal-burning power plants, a major cause of acid rain. The total yearly volume of emissions was mandated to decline 50 percent over twenty years. Underneath the descending cap, existing power plants were given future sulfur-emission permits in proportion to their past pollution. And they were allowed to trade those permits among themselves. Plants that could cheaply reduce their emissions did so and sold their unused permits to those that couldn't. This market-based system was supported by both Republicans and Democrats and backed by President George H. W. Bush. Utilities accepted it because they could profit by selling unused permits. Plus, in their minds, if pollution *did* have to be reduced, a market-based system was preferable to a regulatory one.

The sulfur cap-and-trade program was successful; emissions were reduced faster and at lower cost than expected.[3] So, as concern about climate change mounted in the 1990s, environmentalists, economists, and some polluting corporations began to see cap and trade as a market-friendly way to decrease carbon emissions.

The Clinton administration injected the idea into the 1997 Kyoto Protocol, which, though never ratified by the United States, led to the European carbon trading system. Domestically, the Environmental Defense Fund and the Natural Resources Defense Council formed an alliance with utility companies—the US Climate Action Partnership, or USCAP—to push a cap-and-trade bill through Congress. They recruited Senators Joe Lieberman, a Democrat from Connecticut, and John McCain, a Republican from Arizona, to cosponsor the legislation. Wall Street spotted a potentially lucrative market for trading carbon-based securities and joined in. Former Vice President Al Gore raised and spent millions of dollars on television ads designed to win the public's support. For a brief, shining moment, it seemed as if cap and trade was ready for prime time.

But as all this was happening—indeed, precisely *because* it was happening—the architecture of cap and trade began to morph. The original sulfur model had been simple. Only a few hundred power plants were covered. They all had big, easy-to-monitor smokestacks and were owned by electric utilities whose prices were regulated. Though trading of permits was allowed, it was limited. And though utilities benefited from the system, their gains were in the millions, not billions, of dollars.

Compared with carbon, however, sulfur is a minor pollutant. Carbon is the lifeblood of our economy and a source of billions of dollars in yearly profits for many corporations. Moreover, it flows into our atmosphere not just through a few giant smokestacks but also through countless flues and tailpipes. By acquiring rights to burn carbon in the future, favored companies would collectively gain hundreds of billions of dollars. On top of this, a global market in carbon-based securities would generate substantial profits for traders. Neither of these windfalls, however, is necessary for carbon capping. They occur only if the system creates them.

———

AT THIS POINT, IT'S USEFUL TO UNDERSTAND some details of capping systems. For a ubiquitous substance like carbon, there are four key design questions: (1) Where should the valves (which administer the caps) be located? (2) Should permits be given away or sold? (3) If they're sold, to whom should the proceeds go? (4) Should there be privately created "offsets" that can substitute for government- or trust-issued permits?

Locating the valves.

When there are only a few hundred polluters, each of which can be easily monitored, the logical place to put valves is on each polluter's smokestack. This was the case with sulfur. However, when there are hundreds of millions of polluters, many of them small and mobile, end-of-pipe valves can't catch everything.

Fortunately, there's an alternative: put the valves where the polluting substance enters our economy rather than leaves it. Think of a drip-irrigation system. Typically there's a main water supply with a valve. Then there's an array of thin tubes that emit drops of water next to each plant. If you want to decrease the flow of water, you can put tiny valves in every hole or crank down the big valve at the top. Clearly, it's easier and more effective to turn down the big valve at the top.

The same is true for carbon. If carbon doesn't enter our economy, it can't go out. So putting a few valves upstream makes a lot more sense than putting millions of them downstream.

Actually, an upstream cap doesn't even require physical valves. All it needs is a reporting system applied to the relatively small number of large companies (ExxonMobil, Peabody Energy, El Paso Natural Gas, et al.) that bring fossil fuels into our economy. These first sellers already track the quantities of fuel they sell—how else could they be paid?—and the fuels' carbon content can be calculated from their sales numbers. The companies would then buy, in competitive auctions, one permit for each ton of carbon embedded in the fuels they sell. Once a year they'd "true up" with a supervising entity, much as they do when they pay taxes. If they lacked permits for carbon they sold, they'd pay stiff penalties. All this is pretty easy to do. No physical valves or monitored smokestacks are needed.

Free gift of permits?

Permits to introduce carbon into our economy or atmosphere currently don't exist; they must be created for a carbon cap to work. But these permits are valuable, and the scarcer they get, the more valuable they become. If companies got them for free, they'd reap huge unearned gains. As President Obama's first budget director, Peter

Orszag, put it, "If we don't auction the permits, it would represent the largest corporate welfare program that has ever been enacted in the history of the United States."[4]

Selling carbon permits through competitive bidding is analogous to auctioning drilling rights on public lands. It should be a no-brainer, but there's a political disadvantage: if permits are sold, they can't be used as political bargaining chips. Hence the congressional bias to hand out permits in exchange for support from powerful industries.

Who gets the money?

Assuming that some or all carbon permits are sold competitively, the follow-on question is how to distribute the proceeds. Here two considerations should be borne in mind. One is that the money arises from a gift we all share: our air. The second is that reducing the supply of carbon permits would raise their price, and hence the prices we pay for fossil fuels. Though wealthy households wouldn't feel much pain, low- and middle-income households would. Their purchasing power would decline, and along with it the driving force of our economy. It thus makes sense to return permit revenue to all of us equally.

Should there be offsets?

In the sulfur cap-and-trade program, the only things that can be traded are sulfur permits issued by the government. That means total pollution can't exceed the number of permits. An equally airtight system would make sense for carbon. But airtightness isn't always sought in Washington; in fact, our lawmakers frequently prefer loopholes. Hence the rise of carbon "offsets."

Sometimes offsets and permits are lumped together, but they're not the same. Offsets aren't issued by government, and they're not permits to pollute. Rather, they are privately created claims that a quantified reduction of greenhouse gases has been or will be achieved. And, as with all financial derivatives, there are many varieties of them.

The most familiar are the ones you can buy when you take an airplane trip. If you pay a little extra, you can theoretically offset your share of the flight's carbon emissions. This can occur, say, if your extra payment is used to plant trees. Such voluntary acts of guilt assuagement are unrelated to carbon capping. They may or may not do any good, but at least they do no physical harm.[5] The only risk they carry is that you'll waste your money.

A much greater danger lies with offsets that are included in cap-and-trade programs. Using such offsets, polluters—while continuing to pollute—can claim that the offsets they've purchased result in the same reductions as would have occurred if they'd cut their own pollution. The flavor of this game is aptly captured by a British website called CheatNeutral.com. "Are you a cheater?" the site asks. "We can help you offset your indiscretions by funding someone else to be faithful." The site calls this "cheat offsetting" and brokers deals between loyal and disloyal couples.

If you think this is mere satire, consider what actually happened under the European carbon trading system, launched in 2005 in accordance with the Kyoto Protocol. The European program allows offsets purchased internationally to be substituted for permits issued by the European Union. Over 80 percent of the offsets purchased have involved the destruction of a refrigerant byproduct, HFC-23, that's a potent greenhouse gas. Thanks to offsets, this by-product can be worth five times as much as the refrigerant itself. Many Chinese and Indian firms—plus the brokers who bring their deals to Europe—have gotten rich by making HFC-23 for the sake of destroying it. Meanwhile, European companies that buy the offsets continue to pollute. According to the EU's Commissioner for Climate Action, Connie Hedegaard, the offsets suffer from "a total lack of environmental integrity."[6]

Of course, not all offsets are so questionable, but if the demand for offsets were to rise substantially—if, say, the United States were to accept them under a cap-and-trade regime—you can be sure that the supply of dubious ones would rise as well.[7]

—————

BY NOW IT SHOULD BE CLEAR that not all carbon-capping systems are equal—their structure affects the flow of billions of tons of carbon and potentially trillions of dollars. The starkest contrast is between a downstream system that gives away permits and allows offsets, and an upstream system that auctions all permits, allows no offsets, and returns the revenue to everyone equally. For the sake of discussion, let's call the former *cap and giveaway* and the latter *cap and dividend*. (Full disclosure: I advised members of Congress on the design of a cap-and-dividend system.)

The premise of cap and dividend is that the atmosphere belongs to everyone equally. Its central formula — from all according to their use of the atmosphere, to all in equal share — rests on that premise. But cap and dividend has other virtues: its cap doesn't leak, and it's good for the middle class.

Cap and dividend can be thought of as a rent-recycling system: it makes everyone pay to use our atmosphere but arranges things so that we pay ourselves as co-owners. As a result, when carbon — or, more precisely, air — prices rise, so (automatically) does the money everyone gets back. How people fare as individuals then depends on their own behavior. The more carbon they burn, directly or through the products they buy, the more they pay. But since everyone gets the same amount back, people gain if they conserve and lose if they guzzle. This creates precisely the right individual incentives. It also favors the poor, who of necessity burn the least carbon.

This rent-recycling system has political as well as economic advantages. It's no secret that Americans hate high fuel prices. But when higher fuel prices also bring higher dividends, there'll be a large constituency — indeed, a majority of the population — that benefits from the trade-off. As figure 8.1 shows, dividends

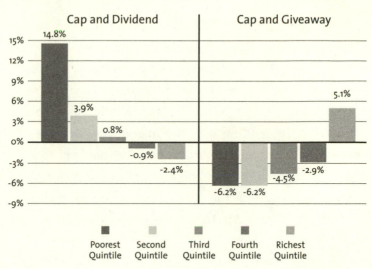

Figure 8.1:
DISTRIBUTIONAL EFFECTS OF CARBON-CAPPING SYSTEMS[8]

benefit the poor and middle class, while giveaways benefit only the rich. This occurs because the rich spend more (per capita) on fossil fuels than the rest of us and own most of the stock in the corporations that would get free permits.

One further virtue of cap and dividend is its transpartisan appeal. Liberals can like it because it stabilizes the climate while benefitting the poor and the middle class. Conservatives can like it because it doesn't expand government, regulate businesses, or pick winners and losers. It simply modifies the rules by which the market operates.

THINK BACK NOW TO 2008. Barack Obama campaigns for president saying, "Generations from now, we will be able to look back and tell our children that . . . this was the moment when the rise of the oceans began to slow and our planet began to heal."[9] Specifically, he proposes to install a descending cap on carbon that will cut US emissions 80 percent by 2050. He also pledges to auction all permits and return 80 percent of the proceeds to the people, spending the rest on clean energy and jobs. Though the details are fuzzy, his proposal sounds a lot like cap and dividend.

Then, in 2009, with Obama in the White House and Democrats in control of both houses of Congress, the legislative process begins. Representative Henry Waxman of California joins with then-Representative Ed Markey of Massachusetts (now a senator) to draft a climate bill and get it passed. Both congressmen are longtime environmentalists. In 2008, Markey introduced a carbon-capping bill that would have auctioned 94 percent of permits and returned half the revenue to low- and moderate-income families. "The atmosphere is a sacred public trust that belongs to all of us," he declared at the time.[10] Its use shouldn't "enrich corporate polluters at consumers' expense."

A year later, as lobbyists engulf Capitol Hill, Waxman and Markey decide to align with the USCAP. The architecture of their bill won't be as Obama proposes, with 100 percent auctions and rebates to the middle class. Instead, permits will be given free to utilities and manufacturers, and polluters will be allowed to continue polluting by buying offsets. Waxman and Markey believe this is the best way to win votes, and Markey's press secretary asks me to remove his earlier statement from my website.

Representative Chris Van Hollen of Maryland sees things differently. He heads the Democratic Congressional Campaign Committee, responsible for getting Democrats elected. He introduces a twenty-five-page cap-and-dividend bill that would auction all permits and return the revenue as equal dividends to every American with a Social Security number. For a majority of Americans, the dividends would exceed their higher energy costs, thus putting money in middle-class pockets. Van Hollen believes this will boost Democrats in swing districts.

Van Hollen's bill languishes in the House Ways and Means Committee while the Waxman-Markey bill passes the Energy and Commerce Committee, which Waxman chairs. Waxman makes deals with coal- and farm-state congressmen, and on June 29, 2009, Speaker Nancy Pelosi rushes his bill to the floor. By now the legislation is over fourteen hundred pages long, and only a few insiders understand it. No matter. After heated debate and behind-the-scenes deals, it squeaks through the House by seven votes.

What passes is later summarized by Representative Rick Boucher, a Democrat from Virginia's coal country, this way:

> I spent two months in intense negotiations to make [the bill] acceptable for coal-fired utilities. I was able to achieve that by providing free allowances [permits], as opposed to having the allowances auctioned, and by providing two billion tons of offsets on an annual basis throughout the life of the program — so coal-fired utilities could simply pay others to reduce emissions, by planting trees, for example, and take full credit for those emission reductions.[11]

After Waxman's victory in the House, the action shifts to the Senate. Again there are two bills: a USCAP measure cosponsored by Senators John Kerry and Joseph Lieberman, and a cap-and-dividend bill cosponsored by Senators Maria Cantwell and Susan Collins, the lone Republican to support carbon capping in any form. As in the House, the polluter-friendly bill gets most of the attention. But it fails to win the backing of enough Democrats or a single Republican, and it is withdrawn before coming to a vote. As it goes down, so does all climate legislation, including cap and dividend.

WHAT WENT WRONG? The postmortems offer several explanations: Obama's lackluster leadership, the economic downturn, the Tea Party rebellion. No doubt all were factors. But the deeper problem is that inside-the-Beltway deal-making isn't enough to pass laws that fundamentally change the US economy. Massive public pressure is needed, and that can't happen when the legislation rewards corporations at the expense of the middle class. As Bill McKibben, the author and climate activist, put it, "We need a movement, and we need something a movement can get behind."[12]

In a recent study, Harvard political scientist Theda Skocpol echoed this analysis.[13] She compared what happened to carbon capping with what happened to health care reform during the same period. Both issues were contested bitterly, both pitted reformers against powerful industries, and both were cliff-hangers until their end. But health reform passed and carbon capping didn't, and Skocpol attributes the contrary outcomes to different depths and intensities of public support.

In the climate battle, the big environmental groups, though well funded, didn't match the grassroots intensity of their opponents. The anticapping campaign, though funded by fossil fuel companies, was fanned by the fact that in the absence of dividends, cap and trade would impose a financial burden on the middle class. It was a "light switch tax," its critics rightly charged, and Tea Party activists angrily attacked it. The resulting furor was a major reason why no Republican senator dared to vote for cap and trade.

On the procapping side, there was no equivalent grassroots upsurge. The big environmental groups had their online petitions and sign-on letters, but these were mostly inch-deep. Neither anger nor fervor was there.

In the health-care battle, no Republican senator voted for reform, either, but on this issue the Democrats held solid. The bill they passed, while not without giveaways, made some form of health insurance available to nearly everyone, regardless of income, employment, or previous health condition. This had been a longtime demand of a well-organized and passionate coalition that included labor, civil rights groups, and churches, and they got most of what they fought for. "Policies ordinary Americans can understand," Skocpol concludes, "policies that deliver concrete benefits to ordinary families, plus the construction of far-reaching networks of allied organizations able to push Congress—these are what it will take to pass carbon-capping legislation next time."

Beyond these political lessons, we can draw some important pointers about system design.

Get the architecture right. Since we'll get, at most, only one timely shot at installing a national carbon cap, we'd better do it right the first time. Carbon trading with free downstream permits and huge quantities of offsets isn't that. At best it replaces one market malfunction—a zero price for polluting—with two others—a porous cap and heightened inequality. What it doesn't do is assure that we'll meet any science-based carbon target on time: the caps are too leaky and public support for them will fade once fuel prices rise noticeably. By contrast, if we cap carbon with auctioned upstream permits and dividends, and without offsets, we'll have a leakproof system popular enough to last.

Keep it simple. Simplicity (as in the thirty-five-page Social Security Act) now seems passé in Washington; thousand-page bills are the norm. That's not because the world is more complex; it's because lobbyists drive legislative language. So beware of any carbon-capping bill that's longer than fifty pages—or can't be explained in a few sentences.

Benefit the many rather than the few. Because fossil fuels are ubiquitous in our economy, any system that raises their prices will necessarily affect everyone's pocketbooks. The danger is that, because a small percentage of Americans owns most of America's corporate stock, they'll gain from higher carbon prices at everyone else's expense. Any carbon-capping system should therefore be designed to benefit the many who share the atmosphere rather than the few who own polluting companies. The best way to do that is with universal dividends that rise automatically as permit prices do.

Speaking more broadly, linking nature's well-being to that of our middle class is the key to harmonizing capitalism with nature. If that connection isn't made, nature's rent can't rise very much, and markets will continue to overuse her.

THE DEFEAT OF CARBON CAPPING IN 2010 has rekindled interest in carbon taxing. As noted earlier, the idea of taxing pollution—or any activity that externalizes costs to society—was first proposed nearly a century ago by British economist Arthur Pigou. It's akin to taxing alcohol and tobacco with the goal not of eliminating them—

prohibition is the way to do that—but of discouraging them, while at the same time raising revenue for government.

Though the idea of taxing carbon has been around a long time, it hasn't gotten far in practice. A modest carbon tax has been enacted in a few countries (Sweden, Norway, Australia) and one Canadian province (British Columbia), with modest results. The furthest the idea has gone in the United States was in 1993, when President Bill Clinton tried to win approval of a small tax on fuel energy content. A bill passed the House but was crushed in the Senate by the oil and coal industries. Since then, the idea has languished in political limbo.

Revived interest in taxing carbon is partly due to the determination of Republicans to cut personal and corporate income taxes. Of all potential revenue sources, a carbon tax strikes many conservatives as among the least objectionable. This leads some pundits to believe that a "grand bargain" is possible around a carbon tax, with liberals backing it for environmental reasons and conservatives accepting it if it allows other taxes to be cut.

Like an upstream cap with all permits auctioned, a carbon tax would be collected from the first sellers of carbon-based fuels and would be simple to administer. Consumers would pay it indirectly because the price of goods they buy would rise in proportion to the amount of carbon used to produce them.

In any plan to tax carbon, the tricky question is what to do with the revenue. One possibility—the conservative favorite—is to cut corporate and personal income taxes. Some liberals support a tax shift but would prefer to cut payroll rather than income taxes.[14] Another possibility is to earmark carbon revenue for specific purposes such as investments in clean energy.

Of all the possible ways to structure a carbon tax, the most beneficial to the middle class is what climatologist James Hansen, its leading proponent, calls "fee and dividend." A fee in this case is a tax with a friendlier name. A dividend in this instance is the same as it is under cap and dividend—an equal payment to everyone. "The only way the public will allow a continually rising carbon price is if the money goes directly back to them, so they can deal with the higher prices," Hansen says.[15]

While I wholeheartedly support the dividend side of fee and dividend, I'm unconvinced that, from nature's point of view, a fee is better than a leak-proof upstream cap. A strict quantitative limit on the amount of carbon entering our economy, with all permits auctioned and no offsets allowed (as in the Van Hollen and Cantwell bills), is by far the best way to cut carbon emissions deeply. In rejecting this mechanism, Hansen and others are reacting to cap and trade's manifold flaws by throwing out the healthy baby with the dirty bathwater.

The fundamental problem with a carbon tax or fee, even if accompanied by dividends, is that it can't guarantee that deep cuts in carbon use will occur. A fee is, after all, merely a signal, not a physical limit, and for highly addictive substances like alcohol, tobacco, and fossil fuels, signals aren't enough. Moreover, a carbon tax is only one factor in the price of fossil fuels; it can easily be lost in the fluctuations of other factors. Think of the recent plunge in natural gas prices due to hydraulic fracturing. And imagine what might happen if similar breakthroughs in oil recovery or discovery occur.

Further, even if a carbon tax pushes the total price of fossil fuels upward, no one knows how high the tax needs to be to reduce emissions to a safe level. That means the only way to proceed is by trial and error. Congress would have to take a first stab, and if that didn't do the job, as is likely, it would have to take another. This might need to happen several times. Given Congress's present inability to do anything sensible on taxes or climate change, it seems unwise to bet the planet on Congress's being sensible on both issues multiple times.

There's one other problem with relying on price alone to reduce total carbon use. The oil-price shock of 1973 prodded America to improve energy efficiency but not to reduce energy consumption. This was a demonstration of the so-called Jevons Paradox, first noticed by British economist William Stanley Jevons in 1865. Jevons observed that improvements in the efficiency of coal use led to greater consumption of coal in a wide range of industries, an increase that more than offset the savings from efficiency. In the twenty-first century, it's quite possible that more people using fossil fuels more efficiently for more purposes (such as the Internet) could still increase total use, or at least dampen the rate at which usage declines. The only way to assure a large decline in aggregate carbon use is to physically crank down the amount that flows through our economy.[16]

Beyond these technical arguments, there's a deeper case for cap and dividend that has to do with the broader changes we need to make in our economic system. To make capitalism tilt toward nature and the middle class, we need new pipes with new forms of property income flowing through them. Cap and dividend would create such pipes and show they can work. A carbon tax wouldn't.

————

WHILE CAP AND TRADE WAS FLOUNDERING in Washington, it was quietly making headway in California, America's most populous state. Arnold Schwarzenegger, the Republican governor, worked closely with a Democratic legislature to pass a bill in 2006 known as the Global Warming Solutions Act, or AB 32 for short. The law committed California to return to its 1990 level of carbon emissions by 2020 and instructed the California Air Resources Board (CARB) to find the most cost-effective ways to do that. CARB hired experts, held hearings, and eventually came up with a list of measures to reach the goal. Cap and trade was one of them, and in 2013 it went into effect.

California's cap-and-trade system is patterned after the Waxman-Markey bill that passed the US House of Representatives. It includes some auctions, but most of the initial permits are given for free to historic polluters. Offsets are also allowed.

But a funny thing happened after CARB's initial giveaway of permits. The California Public Utilities Commission (CPUC)—an entirely different agency that regulates privately owned utilities—decided that the value of the permits given for free by CARB to utilities didn't actually belong to them. Rather, it belonged to the people of California. So the CPUC ordered the utilities to *sell the permits they'd been given and return 100 percent of the proceeds to their customers*. More than that, it ordered them to pay equal "climate dividends" to their residential customers. And this is now happening.

Albeit little noticed, this is a historic development. Because of "the public nature of the atmospheric sink," the CPUC said, utilities must distribute the atmosphere's rent to the people. This is "consistent with the idea that the atmosphere is a commons to which all individuals have an equal claim."[17]

As it turns out, California's climate dividends aren't perfect. They show up as twice-yearly credits on customers' utility bills, where they're hard to notice, rather than as cash in people's bank accounts. (This may change in the future, the CPUC says.) And they're not precisely one person, one share—the best the CPUC can do within its legal authority is one meter, one share.

Still, here's the important thing: this is the first time an American government agency has declared the atmosphere a commons owned by everyone in equal share. Thomas Paine would be proud.

From Here to the
Adjacent Possible

*Only a crisis —actual or perceived—produces real change.
When that crisis occurs, the actions that are taken depend on
the ideas that are lying around.*

—Milton Friedman

Building a dividend system as proposed here is well within America's financial and technical capabilities. The ingredients to do it lie at hand. The organizing principles are over two centuries old and have been road tested in Alaska. Our challenge now is to scale the concept to a meaningful size.

That said, the current political environment makes such scaling all but impossible. It therefore behooves us to take a longer view.

As Charles Darwin and Alfred Russel Wallace noted in the nineteenth century, living systems evolve through a process of variation and selection. Many nonliving systems, including economies, evolve in a similar way. Capitalism in particular has been characterized as a system of "creative destruction."[1]

One aspect of evolution that remained unclear for decades after Darwin and Wallace was whether the vary-and-select process proceeds gradually or in sudden bursts. In theory, it could work either way, but in 1972, paleontologists Niles Eldredge and Stephen Jay Gould published a landmark paper that argued, based on fossil records, that "the history of evolution is not one of stately unfolding, but a story of homeostatic equilibria, disturbed only rarely by rapid and episodic events of speciation."[2] They called this pattern *punctuated equilibrium*, and it seems to apply not only to biological systems but to others as well.

The reason for this punctuated pattern seems to be that complex systems live *near* equilibrium but never quite *at* it. They hover in a zone between equilibrium and chaos, and every once in a while a crisis pushes them toward (or over) the chaotic edge. At such times, they either collapse or shift into what biologist Stuart Kauffman calls the "adjacent possible."[3]

The adjacent possible isn't simply whatever happens next. Rather, it's a set of potential futures in which modified versions of the existing system lurk. *Which* of these versions eventually emerges is inherently unpredictable. But when the system includes humans, it's possible for humans to affect the outcome. We can do this by imagining a preferred future and building support for it prior to the crisis.

It's important to distinguish between the adjacent possible and what might be called the *incremental possible*. By the latter I mean adjustments to the existing system that don't require a serious crisis (aka a punctuation). Political debate in Washington rarely goes beyond this sort of possibility. The adjacent possible, by contrast, lies further in the future and requires a punctuation.

It's often said that pragmatists deal with the incremental possible while idealists fantasize about the adjacent possible. I don't see it that way. I see preparing for the adjacent possible as a different form of pragmatism, a kind that looks further ahead. At certain times in history, it's not fantasy to think about adjacent possibilities — it's pragmatic, strategic, and necessary. Now is such a time.

In my mind, a market economy with liberty and dividends for all is a plausible adjacent possibility. I also believe that a crisis — more severe than that of 2008 — isn't far away and that we need to prepare for it. In the rest of this chapter, I show how we might do so.

THE MOST IMPORTANT WAY TO PREPARE for the next crisis is to *think and act like co-owners of shared wealth*. Jay

Hammond did this, and so should we. I guarantee that if we do, mental and political breakthroughs will follow.

Among the mental breakthroughs that will follow are these:

Old idea: Jobs for all.
Breakthrough: Nonlabor income for all.

The idea that able humans ought to work for a living is age-old, and long may it endure. Less venerable but equally compelling is the idea that there ought to be jobs for everyone. Without rejecting either notion, however, we can—and must—move beyond them.

Work serves economic and, just as important, psychological needs. It's a source not only of income but also of dignity and sometimes happiness. This doesn't mean, however, that work is the *only* source of income, dignity, or happiness. Income can also flow from nonlabor sources, as can dignity and happiness. The point is, our right to pursue dignity and happiness shouldn't be limited by the wages paid in our economy. There's a need for decent-paying jobs for everyone—a need that's increasingly difficult to fill—*and* a need for nonlabor income for all, a need that's considerably easier to fill.

Supplemental nonlabor income is needed today not only because jobs pay less, but also because their *form* has changed. In the last half of the last century, the typical middle-class job was with a long-term employer that provided health insurance and defined-benefit pensions. Such jobs are now scarce. A rising number of jobs are now part-time and temporary, and workers must often stitch two or three together to make ends meet. At the same time, defined-benefit pensions have been replaced by 401(k) plans that put retirement savings at the mercy of the stock market.

In effect, large numbers of workers have become solo navigators of volatile labor and financial markets. They must constantly reinvent themselves and become savvy (or lucky) investors as well. In such an unsteady environment, a reliable base of nonlabor income is a necessity rather than a luxury.

Old idea: One person, one vote.
Breakthrough: One person, one share.

In *Baker v. Carr*, decided in 1962, the Supreme Court ruled that historical and geographic factors couldn't be used to deprive citizens of equal weight in voting. Citing the Fourteenth Amendment's guarantee of equal protection, the court held that all electoral districts must contain roughly the same number of voters.[4] The only exception is the US Senate, where—because of our Constitution—each state gets two senators regardless of the state's population.

A similar formula can apply to income from co-owned wealth. We could divide such income based on unequal criteria, as Alaska at first tried to do; but in *Zobel v. Williams*, decided in 1982, the Supreme Court found such classifications suspect, also because of our Constitution's equal-protection clause. This means that the default formula for distributing income from co-owned wealth is one person, one share.[5]

The *Zobel* decision was a leap for equality from the
political realm to the economic. It's important to note,
however, that the court didn't *require* states to pay equal
dividends from co-owned wealth. It said only that *if* a
state distributes income from co-owned wealth, it must
do so in a nondiscriminatory way. This was a big step
forward, but not as far as we need to go.

The next breakthrough is to affirm a right to receive
income from co-owned wealth, a right that government
would seek to enforce. Such a right would descend from
our equality of birth and our inalienable right to pursue
happiness.

Old idea: Social insurance.
Breakthrough: Shared wealth dividends.

Contributory social insurance was one of the great
achievements of the twentieth century. It mitigated many
of the risks of modern life by including everyone in universal insurance pools. Without it, the suffering caused
by unemployment, old-age poverty, sickness, and disability would be far greater than it is today.

But social insurance goes only so far. Essentially, it's a
safety net that provides some backup when you're retired,
unemployed, or ill, but it does nothing to sustain middle-
class families when wages sink. For that we need a reliable
nonlabor income flow that supplements labor income.

The best way to provide that flow is with dividends
from co-owned wealth. Every American would get the
dividends wired to his or her bank account or debit card.

The amount of the dividends would vary from year to year depending on the income earned during the year. Total dividends would never exceed that income.

In an age of declining real wages, shared wealth dividends would be an essential prop for our middle class. But they'd be more than that. Like social insurance, co-owned wealth dividends would connect Americans to each other and across generations. They'd be an affirmation that Americans belong to a society in which joint inheritances and productivity gains benefit everyone. As Lou Dobbs put it, American citizenship would be worth real money.

Old idea: Redistribution.
Breakthrough: Pre-distribution.

Under the present design of capitalism, differences are magnified and wealth flows inexorably upward. The remedy we usually hear about is redistribution — Robin Hoodish transfers from those with the most money to those with the least. Traditional welfare programs are based on this kind of transfer.

The problem with redistribution is that it begins with a taking of income previously received. This naturally breeds resentment among those whose money is taken. Pre-distribution, by contrast, involves no takings. Rather, it seeks a better-balanced initial distribution of income by the market. As Yale political scientist Jacob Hacker has put it, "Market reforms that encourage a more equal distribution of rewards before government collects taxes

or pays benefits . . . are both more popular and more effective than after-the-fact mopping up."[6]

Achieving that better initial distribution, though, requires a new set of pipes and property rights. In addition
to our existing set, which inexorably skews income upward, we need a second set that distributes some nonlabor income evenly. The *everyone-gets-a-share* pipes would
offset the wealth-concentrating effect of *winner-take-all*
pipes. The relative sizes of the two sets of pipes would
determine the market's overall distribution of income.

Alaska is an example of how pre-distribution can
work, but not the only one. Consider also professional
sports, a $25 billion industry in the United States.[7] Most
income for the industry comes from two sources: ticket
sales and television. But the untempered playing field
is uneven: teams in large media markets have a huge
advantage over teams in small ones. Without a mechanism for sharing some income evenly, large market teams
would overwhelm all the others, and the entire industry
would suffer.

To avoid this, major professional sports leagues have
added mechanisms to even things out. One of these is
the player draft preference given to losing teams; another is revenue sharing. Thus, in the National Football
League, all television revenue — regardless of where it
comes from — is divided equally among all teams.[8] This
enables little Green Bay, Wisconsin, to stand shoulder-
to-shoulder with big New York City, and it makes the
industry as a whole more profitable than it otherwise
would be.

The same kind of dual revenue flow would benefit our national economy. One stream of nonlabor income would flow, as now, disproportionately to a few, while another would be shared equally. Such parallel piping would not only help our middle class; it would also keep our economy chugging, with considerably less inequality and debt than we have now.

———

SO FAR, I'VE TALKED ABOUT CONCEPTUAL breakthroughs. They're a prerequisite for system change, but not sufficient. Eventually, we have to translate transformative ideas into new economic realities—which in this case means new pipes and property rights.

To assist in this post-conceptual work, I suggest we create two to-do lists, one labeled "Things to Do After the Next Crisis" and the other "Things to Do Before the Next Crisis." On the first list I'd place the most important institutions to create after a punctuation: a national dividend-paying fund similar to Alaska's, and legally accountable agents that protect and charge for use of natural and social systems.

On the "Before the Next Crisis" list I'd place all the work we need to do to pave the way for such post-crisis institutions. This includes devising more ways to collect rent from co-owned wealth, legal and economic research supporting those methods, draft legislation, state and regional initiatives, and more educational materials, including that Monopoly-like game I started but didn't finish.

Some of these efforts are already happening. In Vermont, legislators are considering a bill to create a state Common Assets Trust that would earn income from pollution permits, groundwater extraction, and other fees. A research team at the University of Vermont estimated that the trust could pay dividends to every state resident of about $2,000 a year.[9] This is despite the fact that, unlike Alaska, Vermont has no oil or natural gas.

In North Carolina, a band of Cherokees elected to pay half the profits of a tribally owned casino to its members in equal dividends, which last year totaled close to $8,000 per person.[10] An epidemiologist studying children in the area found that within five years, the number of Cherokee living below the poverty line declined by half, and the frequency of behavioral problems among children who moved out of poverty declined by 40 percent.[11]

Further west, in Sherman County, Oregon, residents are reaping a windfall from the wind itself. Using taxes and fees on several large wind farms, the county pays a yearly dividend of $590 to every household. "It's modeled after Alaska," says the county judge, adding that the county can afford to pay more but keeps the checks under $600 to spare its clerks from filing hundreds of federal tax forms.[12]

Other imaginative ideas are abroad. Tech visionary Jaron Lanier writes that Google, Facebook, and other "Siren Servers" have turned a magnificent piece of public infrastructure—the Internet—into a private rent-collecting machine, without paying to use the machine or compensating those whose data and attention they profit from. "Ordinary people 'share,' while elite network presences generate unprecedented fortunes," he observes. Lanier thinks the Siren Servers should pay for our personal information and mind time, though he doesn't say how.[13] One possibility is to charge tiny fees for every ad click and put that money into the dividend pot.

Other countries are experimenting, too. Dozens have created what are generically called *sovereign wealth funds*, which together own more than $6 trillion in assets. The largest of these, in Norway, has assets in excess of $1 million per Norwegian.[14] If it paid dividends of 4 percent, everyone in Norway would receive about $40,000 a year. That, no doubt, seems excessive to Norwegians, so the fund pays 4 percent to their government instead. Norwegians are happy to fund their government this way because it provides, among other things, free medical treatment.

Elsewhere in Europe, there's growing interest in a universal guaranteed income. In 2013, organizers from fifteen countries launched an initiative to get the European Commission to "explore the feasibility" of an EU-wide basic income "high enough to ensure an existence in dignity." Such income would be in addition to, not in lieu of, existing social programs. The organizers fell short of the one million signatures needed but plan a second drive shortly.[15]

Meanwhile, in Switzerland (which isn't part of the EU), organizers obtained enough signatures to put on the ballot an initiative that, if passed, would pay every citizen a monthly stipend of $2,800, financed by an increase in Switzerland's value added tax. The referendum must be held before 2018.[16]

European interest in universal income is driven by attitudes that are stronger there than here: a sense of social solidarity and a belief in individual dignity as a human right. On top of that, there are EU-specific reasons for dividends. Europeans need to "perceive very tangibly that the European Union does something for all of them, not only for the elites," writes Belgian political scientist Philippe van Parijs. "Bismarck helped secure the legitimacy of his unified Germany by creating the world's first public pension system. If the European Union is to be more in people's eyes than a heartless bureaucracy, it will need a universal Euro-Dividend."[17]

Other candidates for dividends are countries with exceptionally large oil deposits. After the United States invaded Iraq in 2003 and deposed its leader, Saddam Hussein, two US senators, Mary Landrieu of Louisiana and Lisa Murkowski of Alaska, pressed the Bush administration to consider an Iraqi Permanent Fund similar to Alaska's.[18] The idea was to unite all Iraqis, regardless of ethnic group, and minimize the risk of a future oil-funded dictatorship. Secretary of State Colin Powell is said to have liked the idea, but for unknown reasons it wasn't pursued.

More recently, experts have suggested the Alaska model for countries that are potential (or actual) victims of the "resource curse," the oft-noted tendency of nations rich in natural resources to be more repressive, corrupt, and slow to develop than others not so well endowed. The best cure for the curse, argue two writers in *Foreign Affairs*, is to "transfer the proceeds from oil directly to the people."[19]

Also notable is a trend among major developing countries—including Mexico, Brazil, and South Africa—to establish direct cash payment programs as alternatives to traditional aid. A book called *Just Give Money to the Poor* concludes that "instead of maintaining a huge aid industry to 'help the poor,' it is better to give money to poor people directly." Contrary to common assumptions, the authors find, most cash recipients use the money wisely—to send their children to school, start businesses, and feed their families.[20]

THE OTHER ITEM ON THE AMERICAN pre-crisis to-do list is to *start, build, and join movements*. Ideas are essential but not enough. Movements put power behind ideas. And on the movement-building front, there's lots of work to do.

The labor movement has been around in various forms for 150 years; it can justly be credited with enlarging our middle class enormously. In recent years, however, as the middle class has waned, so has the power of labor unions. They're still the middle class's strongest agent, but they're no longer strong enough to reshape our economy. They—and the middle class—need allies.

It should be noted that labor unions, by their very nature, focus on labor income. During the cap-and-trade battle, they supported handouts to polluters rather than dividends for all because they believed that polluters would preserve, if not create, jobs in previously organized industries (coal mining, steel, manufacturing). By contrast, the American Association of Retired Persons (AARP) supported dividends because their thirty-five million members understand and rely on nonlabor income.

To be sure, labor unions and AARP agree more often than they disagree, but their divergence over dividends reflects a deeper problem. The middle class as a whole lacks a sense of identity. It's split into subgroups—workers in various industries, seniors, students, farmers, minorities, and so on—each of which identifies more with its own agenda than with a unifying goal. This makes the middle class extremely difficult to organize.

On top of this, our middle class hasn't figured out what its problem is. It knows it's declining and worries about its children's future. But as to the cause of its descent, not to mention the remedy, it remains confused. Yes, more good-paying jobs would be nice, and maybe more public spending or tax cuts would help create them. But the thought that good-paying jobs might never come back in numbers hasn't yet penetrated. Nor have many, outside of Alaska, considered the possibility of dividends. It's easier to blame politicians (or China, or immigrants) than to think these questions through.

It's hard to imagine how a powerful middle-class movement can be built in these circumstances. Still, a look back to the 1930s offers some hope. In 1933, several years after our economy crashed, an unknown doctor named Francis Townsend wrote a letter to the Long Beach *Press-Telegram* proposing to pay pensions of $200 a month to every retired person over sixty. The pensions would be financed by a 2 percent national sales tax and would have to be spent within thirty days. This simple plan, the doctor said, would not only provide security to the elderly but speed up the spending of money, revive the depressed economy, and help everyone.

Much to the doctor's surprise, letters of support poured in. Townsend urged his supporters to set up clubs and send letters to Congress, which they did. Soon the clubs had two million members and were raising money faster than the Democratic Party. Eventually over ten million Americans signed Townsend Plan petitions.[21]

On its surface, the Townsend Plan was about money, but behind it lay a vision of how work and leisure could be balanced in a highly productive economy. The Depression made it clear that there weren't enough jobs for everyone. Townsend's solution was to pay people to retire early, thereby opening jobs to younger entrants. Human life would then be divided into three stages: preparation for labor (youth); labor (midlife); and finally, early and dignified retirement. This vision of a smaller workforce sustained by quickly spent pensions appealed to all age groups.

The Townsend Plan had flaws. For one thing, a 2 percent sales tax wouldn't have raised enough money to pay the proposed pensions. For another, since average wages at the time were around $100 a month, a $200-per-month pension would have been unseemly as well as unaffordable. But there's no doubt that the Townsend movement, along with others led by Upton Sinclair and Huey Long, pushed Congress to pass Social Security in 1935 and expand it in 1939. If such mass movements could be built prior to the Internet, might not comparable ones arise today?

With regard to nature, there are similar possibilities. Today's environmental movement exploded in 1970 when the first Earth Day demonstrations mobilized twenty million people across the country. Soon Richard Nixon was signing laws to protect air, water, and endangered species.

But like the labor movement, the environmental movement has seen its influence wane. In part, this is due to the changing character of environmental problems: global warming is much less visible than oily beaches and flaming rivers. But it's also due to changes in the movement itself. "Even as the environmental movement has become an established presence in Washington, it has become less able to win legislative victories," Nicholas Lemann wrote in the *New Yorker*. "It has concentrated on the inside game, at the expense of broad-based organizing."[22]

As Bill McKibben has said, the environmental movement needs to become a movement again. McKibben's new organization, 350.org, is trying to make it that, using the Internet to connect self-organizing chapters. So far, its focus has been on stopping things, like the

Keystone pipeline, which would bring Canadian tar sand oil to Gulf Coast refineries. But its larger goal—getting the atmosphere's carbon dioxide concentration below 350 parts per million—is indelibly engraved in its name, and its preferred mechanism—charging polluters and paying dividends to all—has the potential to rally broad support.

IN THE PAST, EACH GENERATION of Americans believed it would live better than the one that came before it. That's what we meant by "progress." But though we continue to advance in technological ways, we're no longer progressing in intergenerational betterment. That part of the American dream has died.

Perhaps it can't be saved, and we should just accept that fact. That's what economist Tyler Cowen argues in his 2013 book, *Average Is Over*. Twenty-first-century America will be "much more unfair and much less equal," he says. About ten percent of Americans will be wealthy while the rest grow increasingly poor. Aid from government will be inadequate, and millions will live in shantytowns like those in Mexico and Brazil. On the upside, everyone will enjoy free Wi-Fi and limitless entertainment.[23]

Other plausible futures are even grimmer: climate mayhem, financial collapse, a surveillance state. A strong case can be made that any of these futures is likelier than a middle-class renaissance. Yet it's too soon to throw in the towel. In the darkest days of the Great Depression, with Hitler rising in Germany, John Maynard Keynes wrote an essay called *Economic Possibilities for Our Grandchildren*. Reading it now, in the lifetime of those grandchildren, I'm surprised not only by how hopeful Keynes was but also by how prescient.

Keynes predicted that, barring all-out war, "the standard of life in progressive countries . . . will be between four and eight times as high as it is today," and he was right, even *with* an all-out war. He foresaw that "there will be ever larger . . . groups of people from whom problems of economic necessity have been practically removed," and he was right about that as well.

Keynes was wrong about one thing: the euthanasia of the rentier. Far from being euthanized, rentiers grew more extractive than ever. But perhaps after the next crisis, we'll move in a different direction: instead of euthanizing rentiers, we'll share rent universally. Not extractive rent, but recycled rent that comes from co-owned wealth managed properly.

If Keynes could be optimistic in 1930 and turn out to be largely right, there's room for hope today. As then, there could be terrible horrors before calm and prosperity return, or we could be lucky and suffer only minor horrors. This we can't predict. But there's at least a chance that from a crisis of some proportion, there could emerge an economic system that combines the best of pre-crisis capitalism with the postcrisis adaptations envisioned here.

Is this wild-eyed dreaming? Possibly, but no more so than universal suffrage or social insurance once were. Americans are an adaptive people. If we're willing to shed old ideas and experiment with new ones, there's no telling what we can do.

These are, indeed, times that try our souls, as Thomas Paine wrote about the winter of 1776. But he also wrote, "I know our situation well, and can see the way out of it." And he was right. Perhaps now, as then, we'll find our way out of our current predicaments and into a brighter future.

JOIN THE DISCUSSION

This book is part of a national discussion about universal dividends. If you'd like to join that discussion, please visit www.DividendsForAll.org.

Appendix

THE DIVIDEND POTENTIAL OF CO-OWNED WEALTH

Co-owned wealth is wealth we coinherit or cocreate, wealth of the whole system and/or its subsystems, wealth not created by individuals or businesses. Much of it is truly priceless and should remain that way. However, users of some of it should pay rent, with the income pooled to pay dividends to owners. The question I address here is: Is there enough co-owned wealth that we can plausibly organize this way to pay meaningful dividends to everyone?

To answer this question, we must first establish criteria for choosing assets to rent. The criteria I use are the following:

- The income generated from renting the asset (as opposed to selling it) should be great enough to justify doing so.

- Renting the asset should create benefits beyond dividends. Such ancillary benefits could arise from the internalization of currently externalized costs or from the redirection of extracted rent.

I also make two assumptions:

• Renting is done asset by asset, as political opportunities arise.

• One hundred percent of the rent is distributed in equal dividends to all legal US residents who have a Social Security number.

I now address the question first at the economy-wide level and then by looking at specific assets.

ECONOMY-WIDE

Taken as a whole, rented co-owned wealth would constitute a new sector of our economy. How big would this sector need to be to sustain a large middle class, and is that a plausible size?

As of 2013, approximately three hundred million Americans had Social Security numbers.[1] If each received a dividend of $5,000 yearly, the total revenue needed would be $1.5 trillion, or 9 percent of GDP. This is roughly equivalent to the federal social insurance sector—Social Security, Medicare, disability, and unemployment compensation.[2] It should be noted that co-owned asset rent would not be a cost to our economy, as payments to foreign countries are, but rather would be a circular flow entirely within our economy.

Another comparison is with value added taxes (VATs) in Europe. Though initially paid by businesses, VATs are ultimately paid by consumers; in this way, they're akin to user fees for co-owned assets. There are, however, two significant differences. One is that VATs apply to value added by businesses, whereas co-owned wealth user fees would apply to value added by co-owned assets.[3] The other is that VAT revenue flows to government whereas rent from co-owned wealth would flow to all of us equally.

All countries in the European Union are required to collect VATs; rates range from 20 percent in Britain and France to 25 percent in Sweden. EU-wide, about 13 percent of economic activity consists of public services funded by VATs.[4]

These numbers tell us that in terms of scale, a co-owned wealth dividend sector would be about the size of our present social insurance sector and about 30 percent smaller than the public service sector supported by value added taxes in Europe. Its scale is therefore plausible.

SPECIFIC ASSETS

It's important to note that in considering the revenue potential of specific co-owned assets, numerical precision isn't possible; we're dealing with future projections and many unpredictable variables. What follow are therefore "back of the envelope" calculations made with the best available data.

That said, it's also important to note that, for purposes of this book, numerical precision isn't necessary. My goal is to determine whether annual co-owned wealth dividends in the range of $5,000 per recipient are economically possible if the political will is there. This can be done with rough numbers.

Air

Our atmosphere enriches us in many ways, for which we currently pay nothing. It delivers oxygen for breathing and burning fossil fuels, nitrogen for making fertilizers, fresh water for farming and drinking, waste absorption, ultraviolet protection, and more. Of these services, the most important to charge for—because it causes the most harm—is our use of the atmosphere for carbon absorption.

How much rent might we collect by charging for atmospheric carbon absorption? One way to answer this is to use the formulas in the Carbon Limits and Energy for America's Renewal (CLEAR) Act (Cantwell-Collins, 2009).[5] The bill would require permits for bringing burnable carbon into our economy, gradually reduce the number of yearly permits by 80 percent over 40 years, and require all permits to be purchased at auctions bounded by floor and ceiling prices that would rise over time.

Using the floor and ceiling price formulas contained in the bill, carbon permit revenue in 2033 (twenty years from 2013) would be between $87 billion and $309 billion in 2013 dollars, with a midpoint of $198 billion.

Financial Infrastructure

There's no doubt that everyone benefits from our financial infrastructure, and also no doubt that financial firms and their shareholders benefit far more than anyone else. Yet these firms pay virtually nothing to use that infrastructure. In fact, many of them are subsidized to perform such public functions as creating money.

We might share the benefits of our financial infrastructure more evenly in at least two ways: charge small fees for trading in it, and create new money through dividends rather than bank loans.

Estimates have been made of the revenue that could be generated by a financial transaction tax, which is effectively the same as a financial infrastructure user fee. (The difference is that taxes would flow to government while user fees would flow to the people.) I use a 2012 estimate by Robert Pollin and James Heintz of the University of Massachusetts/Amherst that yields the following revenue (assuming a 50 percent drop from 2011 trading volume as a result of the fees):[6]

Figure A.1: POTENTIAL REVENUE FROM FINANCIAL TRANSACTION FEES

Financial Instrument	Fee Rate	Revenue
Stocks	0.5 percent	$62 billion
Bonds	0.15 percent	$170 billion
Derivatives	0.05 percent	$120 billion
TOTAL		**$352 billion**

Figure 7.1 in chapter 7 uses this $352 billion total (adjusted to $357 billion in 2013 dollars) as the midpoint, with a variance of plus or minus 25 percent for the low and high estimates. I should note that financial transaction fees aren't the only way to make banks and traders pay for using our financial infrastructure. The International Monetary Fund has argued that other measures might work better.[7]

With regard to new money creation: from 2001 to 2008 (before the financial crisis), the average yearly increase in what the Federal Reserve calls M2 was $244 billion.[8] I use this figure (which is adjusted to 2013 dollars) to calculate the low end of the range in figure 7.1. For the high end I use the average annual change in M2 from 2001 to 2013, which includes several years of "quantitative easing." That figure, translated into 2013 dollars, is $323 billion. The middle figure is halfway between.

Intellectual-Property Protection

Intellectual property (IP) rights owned by private corporations include patents, copyrights, and trademarks granted and enforced by the federal government. Such property rights are enormously valuable. A recent study by the Department of Commerce found that IP-intensive industries account for about a third of US GDP.[9] This is the reason why our government goes to such great lengths to protect IP, not only within the United States but worldwide.

That said, it's not simple to estimate how much revenue could be generated by charging for IP protection. According to the Department of Commerce study, the 15 most patent- and copyright-intensive industries (software, entertainment, pharmaceuticals, et al.) accounted for $1.6 trillion of value added in 2010. A 20 percent value added fee on those industries, comparable to Britain's value added tax, would yield $320 billion.

Electromagnetic Spectrum

The economic value of the electromagnetic spectrum — long used for radio and television and increasingly used for cell phones and data transmission — is enormous and rapidly growing. By law, the spectrum is publicly owned, but in practice, much of it has been given or sold to private broadcasting and telecommunications companies. Putting a value on using it is complicated by many factors, including the different properties of different frequencies.

For purposes of figure 7.1, I've adopted a simplified valuation methodology similar to that used for IP protection. According to the US Bureau of Economic Analysis, the value added by the broadcasting and telecommunications industries, averaged over 1998 to 2011, was 2.5 percent of GDP. Applying that to 2013 GDP yields a value added of $418 billion. A 20 percent value added fee on those spectrum-intensive industries would generate $84 billion for dividends.

Other Assets

The list of other co-owned assets that might be rented for dividend purposes includes minerals and timber on public lands (including offshore continental shelves); the Internet (commercial use only); and air, soil, and water as waste sinks for pollutants in addition to carbon. Complexities abound in estimating the revenue such rents might generate; I have therefore omitted them from figure 7.1. However, there is much opportunity for research and revenue in this area.

CONCLUSION

There is sufficient rentable co-owned wealth in America to pay meaningful dividends to everyone.

NOTES

Chapter 1: A Simple Idea

1. Calculations made at http://www.measuringworth.com.

Chapter 2: The Tragedy of Our Middle Class

1. The best Internet source for information about economic inequality in America is http://inequality.org. The data for figure 2.1 (the most recent available) were taken from Edward N. Wolff, "The Asset Price Meltdown and the Wealth of the Middle Class," National Bureau of Economic Research Working Paper No. 18559 (November 2012), table 2, 58.

2. See especially Richard Wilkinson and Kate Pickett, *The Spirit Level: Why Greater Equality Makes Societies Stronger* (New York: Bloomsbury Press, 2009), 49 ff.

3. US Census Bureau, http://www.census.gov/hhes/www/income/data/historical/household/, table H-6, and http://www.census.gov/hhes/www/income/data/historical/people/, table P-8.

4. James Madison, *National Gazette*, March 3, 1792, http://www.brainyquote.com/quotes/authors/j/james_madison.html.

5. Alexis de Tocqueville, *Democracy in America* (1835), Book II, chapter 18, http://xroads.virginia.edu/~Hyper/DETOC/ch2_18.htm.

6. "Chart of the Week: Union Membership Continues to Decline," http://blog.heritage.org/2013/01/27/chart-of-the-week-union-membership-continues-to-decline/.

7. Figure 2.2 is taken from the Congressional Budget Office, "The Distribution of Household Income and Federal Taxes, 2010"

(Washington, DC, 2013), 18, http://www.cbo.gov/sites/default/files/cbofiles/attachments/44604-AverageTaxRates.pdf.

8. Robert Reich, *Aftershock: The Next Economy and America's Future* (New York: Vintage, 2011), 60 ff.

9. Schwartz Center for Economic Policy Analysis, the New School, "Retirement Income Security Fact Sheet" (2012), https://docs.google.com/file/d/0B35b9afh6ZgZODkya0ZOTUl3RXc/edit?pli=1.

10. Figure 2.3 is adapted from C. Brett Lockard and Michael Wolf, *Occupational Employment Projections to 2020*, US Labor Department, Bureau of Labor Statistics, Table 3 (Washington, DC, 2012), http://www.bls.gov/opub/mlr/2012/01/art5full.pdf.

11. Michael Abramowitz and Lori Montgomery, "Bush Addresses Income Inequality," *Washington Post*, February 1, 2007, http://www.washingtonpost.com/wp-dyn/content/article/2007/01/31/AR2007013100879.html.

12. Lawrence Mishel, "The Overselling of Education," *American Prospect*, January 2011, A21.

13. Joyce Appleby, *The Relentless Revolution: A History of Capitalism* (New York: W. W. Norton, 2010), 153.

14. "Robots don't complain, or demand higher wages, or kill themselves," Economist, August 6, 2011, http://www.economist.com/node/21525432.

15. Harold Meyerson, "Back from China?" *American Prospect*, December 2011, 43.

Chapter 3: Fix the System, Not the Symptoms

1. "Pareto principle," Wikipedia, http://en.wikipedia.org/wiki/Pareto_principle.

2. Joshua M. Epstein and Robert L. Axtell, *Growing Artificial Societies: Social Science from the Bottom Up* (Cambridge, MA: MIT Press, 1996).

3. Chuck Collins, *99 to 1: How Wealth Inequality Is Wrecking the World and What We Can Do about It* (San Francisco: Berrett-Koehler Publishers, 2012).

4. Leo Barnes, "The Economic Equivalent of War," *Antioch Review*, Summer 1944.

5. Eugene Smolensky, Sheldon Danziger, and Peter Gottschalk, "Trends in the Well-Being of Children and Elderly Since 1939," Institute for Research on Poverty, University of Wisconsin–Madison, 1987, table 1, p. 7, http://www.ssc.wisc.edu/cde/cdewp/87-22.pdf.

6. "Social Security Administrative Expenses," Social Security Administration, http://www.ssa.gov/OACT/STATS/admin.html.

7. Social insurance as a percentage of the US economy: Social Security and Medicare Boards of Trustees, *A Summary of the 2013 Annual Reports*, http://www.ssa.gov/oact/trsum/; US Department of Labor, Employment and Training Administration, *Financial Data Handbook for 2012*, http://workforcesecurity.doleta.gov/unemploy/hb394/hndbkrpt.asp.

8. FDR quote on payroll taxes: History site of the Social Security Administration, http://www.ssa.gov/history/Gulick.html.

9. *Report of the Committee on Economic Security*, Social Security Administration, Washington, DC, 1934, http://www.ssa.gov/history/reports/ces5.html.

Chapter 4: Extracted Rent

1. Thorstein Veblen, *Absentee Ownership* (New York: B. W. Huebsch, 1923). Citation is from Beacon Paperback edition (Boston, 1967), 13.

2. "The Richest People in America, 2013," *Forbes*, http://www.forbes .com/forbes-400/list/.

3. Janet Lowe, *Warren Buffett Speaks: Wit and Wisdom from the World's Greatest Investor* (New York: John Wiley & Sons, 1997), 164.

4. Herbert Simon, "Public Administration in Today's World of Organizations and Markets," public lecture (2000), http:// research.mbs.ac.uk/hsi/Aboutus/HerbertSimonsLastPublic Lecture.aspx.

5. Adam Smith, *The Wealth of Nations*, chapter 9, "Of the Rent of Land," conclusion (London, 1776), 212, http://www2.hn.psu .edu/faculty/jmanis/adam-smith/wealth-nations.pdf.

6. See my reconsideration of Henry George's *Progress and Poverty* in the *New Republic*, December 11, 1971, http://cooperativeindi-vidualism.org/barnes-peter_reconsideration-of-progress-and-poverty-by-henry-george-1971.html.

7. Smith, *Wealth of Nations*, 213.

8. John Kay, "Powerful interests are trying to control the market," *Financial Times*, November 10, 2009, http://www .ft.com/intl/cms/s/0/113092ee-ce2f-11de-a1ea-00144feabdc0 .html#axzz2qhoM5PwC.

9. Ezekiel J. Emanuel, "Spending More Doesn't Make Us Health-ier," *New York Times*, October 30, 2011, http://opinionator.blogs .nytimes.com/2011/10/27/spending-more-doesnt-make-us-healthier/. In 2009, Canada spent $4,363 per person on health care while the United States spent $7,960.

10. According to economist Dean Baker, America spent close to $300 billion in 2011 on prescription drugs. In the absence of patent monopolies, the same drugs would have cost around $30 billion, an amount that implies a transfer to the pharmaceutical

industry of about $270 billion. Drug companies claim that they use the extra money for research, but in fact they spend far more on marketing than on research. Dean Baker, "Reducing Waste with an Efficient Medicare Prescription Drug Benefit," Center for Economic and Policy Research Issue Brief, Washington, DC, January 2013, http://www.cepr.net/documents/publications/medicare-drug-2012-12.pdf.

11. For an explanation of fractional reserve banking, see "Fractional reserve banking," Wikipedia, http://en.wikipedia.org/wiki/Fractional_reserve_banking.

12. For data on financial-industry profits, see Sameer Khatiwada, "Did the financial sector profit at the expense of the rest of the economy? Evidence from the United States," Discussion paper 206, International Institute for Labour Studies, Geneva, Switzerland, 2010, figure 1, p. 2, http://www.ilo.org/wcmsp5/groups/public/---dgreports/---inst/documents/publication/wcms_192804.pdf. The report finds that "from 1960 to 1984, the financial sector's share of total corporate profit averaged 17.4 percent, but from 1985 to 2008, it averaged roughly 30 percent. From 2001 to 2003, it was above 40 percent, reaching as high as 44 percent in 2002." Regarding bonuses in 2008, see Ben White, "What Red Ink? Wall Street Paid Hefty Bonuses," *New York Times*, January 28, 2009, http://www.nytimes.com/2009/01/29/business/29bonus.html.

13. Adam Shell, "Wall Street bonus pool for 2012 jumps 8% to $20 billion," *USA Today*, February 26, 2013, http://www.usatoday.com/story/money/markets/2013/02/26/wall-street-cash-bonuses-jump-8/1948641/.

14. Joseph E. Stiglitz, "The 1 Percent's Problem," *Vanity Fair*, May 31, 2012, http://www.vanityfair.com/politics/2012/05/joseph-stiglitz-the-price-on-inequality.

15. John Maynard Keynes, *The General Theory of Employment, Interest and Money*, chapter 24, "Concluding Notes" (Basingstoke, UK: Palgrave Macmillan, 1936).

16. Derivatives are discussed in "Heavy Lifting," *Economist*, Aug. 17, 2013, 63, http://www.economist.com/news/finance-and-econo mics/21583698-efforts-reform-vast-and-opaque-market-are-showing-results-heavy-lifting. It cites the Bank for International Settlements as putting the notional value of global derivatives contracts outstanding at the end of 2012 at $687 trillion. See also the quarterly reports on bank trading and derivatives published by the US Office of the Controller of the Currency. The OCC puts the notional value of derivatives held by American banks in 2013 at $231 trillion.

17. Foreign exchange transactions are analyzed by the Bank for International Settlements in its "Triennial Central Bank Survey of Foreign Exchange and Derivatives Market Activity in 2010—Final Results," http://www.bis.org/publ/rpfxf10t.htm. Average *daily* trading that year was around $4 trillion.

Chapter 5: Recycled Rent

1. For a discussion of the sources of common wealth, see Peter Barnes, *Capitalism 3.0: A Guide to Reclaiming the Commons* (San Francisco: Berrett-Koehler Publishers, 2006), 66 ff.

2. Jonathan Rowe et al., *Our Common Wealth: The Hidden Economy That Makes Everything Else Work* (San Francisco: Berrett-Koehler Publishers, 2013), 61.

3. Dallas Burtraw and Samantha Sekar, *Two World Views on Carbon Revenues*, Resources for the Future, Washington, DC (2013), 4, http://www.rff.org/RFF/Documents/RFF-DP-13-32.pdf.

Chapter 6: The Alaska Model

1. Cliff Groh and Gregg Erickson, "The Improbable but True Story of How the Alaska Permanent Fund and the Alaska Permanent Fund Dividend Came to Be," in *Alaska's Permanent Fund Dividend: Examining Its Suitability as a Model*, ed. Karl Widerquist and Michael W. Howard (New York: Palgrave Macmillan, 2012).

2. Todd Moss, ed., *The Governor's Solution: How Alaska's Oil Dividend Could Work in Iraq and Other Oil-Rich Countries* (Washington, DC: Center for Global Development, 2012), 18.

3. *Zobel v. Williams*, 457 US 55 (1982).

4. Moss, *The Governor's Solution*, 23.

5. Alaska Permanent Fund Corporation, statement of revenues, expenditures, and changes in fund balances for the fiscal year ending June 30, 2012, http://www.apfc.org/_amiReportsArchive/APFC201211.pdf.

6. Hammond claims (Moss, *The Governor's Solution*, 51) that Alaska is the only state in which the gap between the haves and the have-nots has narrowed over the last twenty years. Regarding native poverty: the rate in 1980 was 25 percent. See Scott Goldsmith, "The Alaska Permanent Fund Dividend: A Case Study in Direct Distribution of Resource Rent," in Moss, *The Governor's Solution*, 78.

7. Governor Sarah Palin on "Hannity & Colmes," September 18, 2008, http://www.foxnews.com/story/0,2933,424346,00.html.

8. Goldsmith, in Moss, *The Governor's Solution*, 73.

Chapter 7: Dividends for All

1. Robert Theobald, *The Guaranteed Income: Next Step in Socioeconomic Evolution?* (Garden City, NY: Doubleday, 1966); James Tobin, "The case for an income guarantee," *Public Interest*, issue no. 4 (Summer 1966), http://www.nationalaffairs.com/public_interest/detail/the-case-for-an-income-guarantee.

2. Brian Steensland, *The Failed Welfare Revolution: America's Struggle over Guaranteed Income Policy* (Princeton, NJ: Princeton University Press, 2007), 70–78.

3. Milton Friedman, *Capitalism and Freedom* (Chicago: University of Chicago Press, 1962), 192 ff.

4. Center on Budget and Policy Priorities, *Policy Basics: The Earned Income Tax Credit*, http://www.cbpp.org/files/policybasics-eitc .pdf.

5. "Employee Stock Ownership Plan Facts," National Center for Employee Ownership, http://www.esop.org.

6. Louis O. Kelso and Mortimer J. Adler, *The Capitalist Manifesto* (New York: Random House, 1958).

7. Dwight Murphey, *A Shared Market Economy: A Classical Liberal Rethinks the Market System* (self-published, 2009), http://dwight-murphey-collectedwritings.info/SME-TofC-2.htm.

8. Ibid., chapter 3.

9. Bill O'Reilly, "Government intervention in the American oil industry?" *The O'Reilly Factor*, February 24, 2012, http://www .foxnews.com/on-air/oreilly/index.html#/v/1472237953001/government-intervention-in-the-american-oil-industry/?playlist_id=86923.

10. Robert Reich, "Restore the Basic Bargain," November 28, 2011, http://robertreich.org/post/13469691304.

11. For a clear explanation of how this could work, see *The Positive Money System in Plain English*, at http://www.positivemoney.org. See also numerous articles at the American Monetary Institute website, http://www.monetary.org.

12. Irving Fisher, *100% Money*, originally published in the *Economic Forum*, April–June 1936, 406–20, http://www.mondopolitico .com/library/100percent/c1.htm.

13. Milton Friedman, *The Optimum Quantity of Money and Other Essays* (Chicago: Aldine Publishing Co., 1969, chapter 1. See also James Robertson and Joseph Huber, *Creating New Money: A Monetary Reform for the Information Age* (London: New Economics Foundation, 2000), http://www.jamesrobertson.com/book/creatingnewmoney.pdf.

14. Adair Turner, "Debt, Money and Mephistopheles: How Do We Get Out of This Mess?" speech at Cass Business School, February 6, 2013, http://www.fsa.gov.uk/static/pubs/speeches/0206-at.pdf; and Ben Bernanke, "Deflation: Making Sure 'It' Doesn't Happen Here," remarks, November 21, 2002, http://www.federalreserve.gov/boarddocs/speeches/2002/20021121/.

15. Organization for Economic Cooperation and Development, "Average annual hours actually worked per worker," http://stats.oecd.org/Index.aspx?DataSetCode=ANHRS.

Chapter 8: Carbon Capping: A Cautionary Tale

1. John Dales, *Pollution, Property & Prices: An Essay in Policy-Making and Economics* (Toronto: University of Toronto Press, 1968).

2. R. H. Coase, "The Problem of Social Cost," *Journal of Law & Economics* III (October 1960), http://www.econ.ucsb.edu/~tedb/Courses/UCSBpf/readings/coase.pdf. I discuss Coase at some length in *Capitalism 3.0*, p. 58 ff. While I admire Coase and consider his thinking a real breakthrough, I disagree with his contention that it makes no difference whether initial property rights are given to polluters or pollutees. It may not affect the total quantity of pollution, but it assuredly affects the incomes of pollutees and polluters.

3. Environmental Protection Agency, "Cap and Trade: Acid Rain Program Results," http://www.epa.gov/capandtrade/documents/ctresults.pdf.

4. David Wessel, "Pollution Politics and the Climate-Bill Give-away," *Wall Street Journal*, May 23, 2009, http://online.wsj.com/news/articles/SB124304449649349403.

5. Voluntary offsets that do no harm may also do little good. For example, offsets bought by Oscar-attending movie stars in 2007 went to Waste Management Inc. for cleaning up a methane-emitting landfill that the company had already been ordered to fix. *BloombergBusinessweek*, "Another Inconvenient Truth," March 25, 2007, http://www.businessweek.com/stories/2007-03-25/another-inconvenient-truth.

6. "EU plans to clamp down on carbon trading scam," *Guardian*, October 25, 2010, http://www.guardian.co.uk/environment/2010/oct/26/eu-ban-carbon-permits.

7. Some projects financed with offsets are legitimate. If private buyers want to fund them, that's fine. But whatever emissions are avoided by such projects should be in addition to, not in lieu of, real emission reductions achieved through reducing the number of permits. In the ideal scenario, there'd be separate markets for permits and offsets, and offsets would add to, rather than subtract from, the reductions achieved through permit limits.

8. James K. Boyce and Matthew Riddle, *Cap and Dividend: How to Curb Global Warming While Protecting the Incomes of American Families*, Political Economy Research Institute, Working Paper 150, November 2007, figure 5, p. 12, http://www.peri.umass.edu/fileadmin/pdf/working_papers/working_papers_101-150/WP150.pdf.

9. Obama nomination victory speech, http://www.huffingtonpost.com/2008/06/03/obamas-nomination-victory_n_105028.html.

10. Statement of Edward Markey before the House Select Committee on Energy Independence and Global Warming, January 23, 2008, http://www.gpo.gov/fdsys/pkg/CHRG-110hhrg58417/html/CHRG-110hhrg58417.htm.

11. Lewis Peck, "A Veteran of the Climate Wars Reflects On U.S. Failure to Act," *Yale Environment 360*, January 4, 2011, http://e360.yale.edu/feature/a_veteran_of_the_climate_wars_reflects_on_us_failure_to_act/2356/.

12. "Bill McKibben on Building a Climate Action Movement" (interview), *Yale Environment 360*, April 23, 2009, http://e360.yale.edu/feature/bill_mckibben_on_building_a_climate_action_movement/2143/.

13. Theda Skocpol, "Naming the Problem: What It Will Take to Counter Extremism and Engage Americans in the Fight against Global Warming," http://www.scholarsstrategynetwork.org/sites/default/files/skocpol_captrade_report_january_2013y.pdf.

14. The argument for cutting payroll taxes is that it would benefit workers and encourage employers to hire more of them. While the first part of the argument is valid, it overlooks the fact that many people who'd be affected by higher carbon prices—retired workers, students, stay-at-home parents, workers in the underground economy, and the unemployed—don't pay payroll taxes. The second part of the argument, however, is largely specious. Employers hire new workers if and when they need them; a slight reduction in payroll taxes would barely alter their behavior. What a payroll tax cut for employers *would* do is generate windfalls for large employers like Walmart and McDonald's, and weaken the financing of Social Security.

15. Andrew Revkin, "Hansen on Next Climate Steps: Charge Polluters; Pay People," *New York Times*, Dot Earth blog, June 6, 2008, http://dotearth.blogs.nytimes.com/2008/06/06/james-hansen-tax-c02-emitters-pay-citizens/.

16. Hansen makes another argument for a fee: it is, he says, the only sort of carbon pricing that China will adopt, since China is loath to physically limit its growth options. Therefore, he contends,

if we want to sync our carbon price with China's, we'll need to impose a comparable fee. (The purpose of such syncing is to prevent countries with low carbon prices from outcompeting countries with higher ones.) Here again, I agree with part of Hansen's argument but not the whole. Just because China won't cap its carbon use doesn't mean that we shouldn't, or that we can't sync carbon prices if we do. Regardless of how each country sets its carbon prices, they can be synced with border adjustment fees. If one country's carbon price is lower than another's, import fees can make up the difference.

17. California Public Utilities Commission, "Decision Adopting Cap-and-Trade Greenhouse Gas Allowance Revenue Allocation Methodology for the Investor-Owned Electric Utilities, San Francisco," 2012, 58, http://docs.cpuc.ca.gov/PublishedDocs/Efile/G000/M031/K744/31744787.pdf.

Chapter 9: From Here to the Adjacent Possible

1. Joseph Schumpeter, *Capitalism, Socialism, and Democracy* (New York: Harper & Row, 1942).

2. Niles Eldredge and Stephen Jay Gould, "Punctuated equilibria: An alternative to phyletic gradualism," in T. J. M. Schopf, ed., *Models in Paleobiology* (San Francisco: Freeman Cooper, 1972, 82–115, http://www.blackwellpublishing.com/ridley/classictexts/eldredge.pdf.

3. Stuart Kauffman, *Investigations* (New York: Oxford University Press, 2003).

4. *Baker v. Carr*, 369 US 186 (1962).

5. *Zobel v. Williams*, 457 US 55 (1982).

6. The term "pre-distribution" was first used, as best I can determine, by Yale political scientist Jacob Hacker, in a 2011 essay, "The institutional foundations of middle-class democracy,"

which is well worth reading; http://www.policy-network.net/
pno_detail.aspx?ID=3998&title=The+institutional+foundations
+of+middle-class+democracy.

7. W. R. Hambrecht Co., *U.S. Professional Sports Market and Fran-
chise Value Report* (2012), http://www.wrhambrecht.com/wp-con-
tent/uploads/2013/09/SportsMarketReport_2012.pdf.

8. Since the NFL is private and doesn't release financial data, it's
impossible to know exactly how its revenue pie is divided. However, recent large television contracts suggest that television income now exceeds ticket sales. See Daniel Kaplan, "The road to
$25 billion," *SportsBusiness Journal*, http://www.sportsbusiness-
daily.com/Journal/Issues/2013/01/28/In-Depth/NFL-revenue-
streams.aspx.

9. Gary Flomenhoft, ed., *Valuing Common Assets for Public Finance
in Vermont* (Burlington, VT: Gund Institute, University of Vermont, 2008), http://www.uvm.edu/giee/research/greentax/doc-
uments/Valuing_Common_Assets_3_20_final.pdf.

10. Caitlin Bowling, "Cherokee casino hits earning milestone," *Smoky
Mountain News*, May 15, 2013, http://www.smokymountainnews
.com/news/item/10295-cherokee-casino-hits-earning-milestone.

11. Moises Velasquez-Manoff, "What Happens When the Poor Receive a Stipend?" *New York Times*, January 18, 2014, http://opin-
ionator.blogs.nytimes.com/2014/01/18/what-happens-when-
the-poor-receive-a-stipend/.

12. Lee Van Der Voo, "Money Blows in to a Patch of Oregon
Known for Its Unrelenting Winds," *New York Times*, May 30,
2011, http://www.nytimes.com/2011/05/31/us/31wind.html.

13. Jaron Lanier, *Who Owns the Future?* (New York: Simon & Schus-
ter, 2013).

14. Fund rankings, Sovereign Wealth Institute, http://www.sw-finstitute.org/fund-rankings/. Alistair Doyle, "All Norwegians become crown millionaires in oil saving landmark," Reuters, January 8, 2014, http://www.reuters.com/article/2014/01/08/us-norway-millionaires-idUSBREA0710U20140108.

15. European Citizens' Initiative for an Unconditional Basic Income, http://basicincome2013.eu/.

16. Stephan Faris, "The Swiss Join the Fight Against Inequality," *BloombergBusinessweek*, January 16, 2014, http://www.business-week.com/articles/2014-01-16/inequality-fight-swiss-will-vote-on-minimum-income.

17. Philippe van Parijs, "The Euro-Dividend," *Social Europe Journal*, July 3, 2013, http://www.social-europe.eu/author/philippe-van-parijs/.

18. Warren Vieth, "A Fund Could Spread Iraq's Oil Wealth to Its Citizens," *Los Angeles Times*, May 1, 2003, http://articles.latimes.com/2003/may/01/news/war-iraqoil1.

19. Nancy Birdsall and Arvind Subramanian, "Saving Iraq From Its Oil," *Foreign Affairs*, July/August 2004, http://www.foreignaffairs.com/articles/59923/nancy-birdsall-and-arvind-subramanian/saving-iraq-from-its-oil.

20. Joseph Hanlon, Armando Barrientos, and David Hulme, *Just Give Money to the Poor: The Development Revolution from the Global South* (Sterling, VA: Kumerian Press, 2010).

21. Edwin Amenta, *When Movements Matter: The Townsend Plan and the Rise of Social Security* (Princeton, NJ: Princeton University Press, 2006).

22. Nicholas Lemann, "When the earth moved: What happened to the environmental movement?" *New Yorker*, April 15, 2013.

23. Tyler Cowen, *Average Is Over: Powering America Beyond the Age of the Great Stagnation* (New York: Dutton, 2013), 229–30 (Kindle Edition).

Appendix: The Dividend Potential of Co-owned Wealth

1. Assumes 95 percent of US residents are eligible for Social Security and a 2013 population of 316 million; http://www.census .gov/population/foreign/data/acs2003.html.

2. Social Security and Medicare Boards of Trustees, *A Summary of the 2013 Annual Reports*, http://www.ssa.gov/oact/trsum/; US Department of Labor, Employment and Training Administration, *Financial Data Handbook for 2012*, http://workforcesecurity.doleta .gov/unemploy/hb394/hndbkrpt.asp.

3. When applied to nature, co-owned wealth user fees can be thought of as value *subtracted* fees—that is, compensation for harm done. They both internalize and discourage externalities, a benefit that value added taxes don't provide.

4 "European Union value added tax," Wikipedia, http:// en.wikipedia.org/wiki/European_Union_value_added_tax. Philippe van Parijs calculates that an EU-wide dividend of about $3,250 per year would require an increase in EU VAT rates of about 20 percent. *Social European Journal*, July 3, 2013, http://www.social-europe.eu/author/philippe-van-parijs.

5. CLEAR Act text, http://www.cantwell.senate.gov/issues/Leg_ Text.pdf.

6. Robert Pollin and James Heintz, *Transaction Costs, Trading Elasticities, and the Revenue Potential of Financial Transaction Taxes for the United States*, Political Economy Research Institute (Amherst, MA: University of Massachusetts/Amherst, 2011), http://www .peri.umass.edu/fileadmin/pdf/research_brief/PERI_FTT_Re-

search_Brief.pdf. See 2012 update at http://www.peri.umass
.edu/fileadmin/ pdf/ftt/ Pollin--Heintz--Memo_on_FTT_Rates_
and_Revenue_Potential_w_references----6-9-12.pdf.

7. Stijn Claessens, Michael Keen, and Ceyla Pazarbasioglu, *Financial Sector Taxation: The IMF'S Report to the G20*, September 2010, http://www.imf.org/external/np/seminars/eng/2010/paris/pdf/090110.pdf.

8. St. Louis Federal Reserve, "Graph: M2 Money Stock," http://research.stlouisfed.org/fred2/graph/?id=M2.

9. US Department of Commerce, *Intellectual Property and the U.S. Economy* (2012), http://www.esa.doc.gov/sites/default/files/reports/documents/ipandtheuseconomyindustriesinfocus.pdf.

ACKNOWLEDGMENTS

The ideas in this book have evolved over many years and have been inspired (wittingly or not) by many people. My father, Leo Barnes, is probably most responsible: he got me thinking about the structure of economic systems. Other intellectual companions (who are less responsible) include Harriet Barlow, David Bollier, James Boyce, Chuck Collins, Lewis Hyde, Marjorie Kelly, Frances and Anna Lappé, David Morris, Jonathan Rowe, Gary Ruskin, and Susan Witt.

In addition, I've benefited from the counsel of Marcellus Andrews, Dean Baker, Robert Borosage, Peter Brown, Dallas Burtraw, Robert Costanza, Herman Daly, Jane D'Arista, Steven de Canio, Peter Dorman, Richard Douthwaite, Gary Flomenhoft, John Fullerton, Mason Gaffney, William Greider, Jon Isham, Ed Kirshner, Dwight Murphey, Richard Norgaard, and Robert Reich.

I want to thank the many people who worked so hard to promote cap-and-dividend legislation, especially George Abar, Sam Boykin, David Fenton, Robert Friedman, Ted Glick, Ann Hancock, Ana Micka, Michael Noble, Bill Parsons, John Passacantando, Robert Perkowitz, Rafe Pomerance, Rick Reed, Amit Ronen, Mike Sandler, Darcy Scott Martin, Betsy Taylor, Mike Tidwell, and Lee Wasserman.

I particularly want to thank Representative Chris Van Hollen and Senators Maria Cantwell and Susan

Collins for introducing cap-and-dividend legislation. They bucked polluting industries and stood up for middle-class families. I hope more political leaders will follow their footsteps in the future.

For first-rate research and editorial assistance, I'm grateful to Seth Zuckerman and Grace Chang. For time to think and write, I'm indebted to the Blue Mountain Center and Ragdale, two outstanding retreats for writers and other artists.

The people most responsible for this book are my wife and partner, Cornelia Durrant, who consistently encouraged me to be bold, and Steve Piersanti, my editor at Berrett-Koehler, who honed the book to its essence. I am deeply grateful to both.

–Peter Barnes
Point Reyes Station, California
January 2014

INDEX

ABOUT THE AUTHOR

Photo by Sarah Hadley

Peter Barnes is a writer and entrepreneur whose work has focused on market-based improvements to capitalism.

Barnes began his career as a correspondent for *Newsweek* and the *New Republic* magazines, writing frequently about economic issues. He then spent two decades as a socially responsible business leader, cofounding a worker-owned solar energy company and Working Assets (now Credo), a financial services and telephone company that has donated over $75 million to progressive nonprofits. In 1996, he returned to writing.

In 2001 and 2006, Barnes published two groundbreaking books on the future of capitalism: *Who Owns the Sky?* and *Capitalism 3.0.* In 2008, he initiated a campaign to limit and auction carbon permits and return the proceeds to all Americans equally, a model first proposed in *Who Owns the Sky?*

Over the years Barnes has served on numerous boards, including the National Cooperative Bank, the California Solar Industry Association, Greenpeace International, and the Center for Economic and Policy

Research. He also founded the Mesa Refuge, a writers' retreat in Point Reyes Station, California.

Barnes has two sons and lives with his wife in Northern California. For more information, visit Peter-Barnes.org.

Also by Peter Barnes

Capitalism 3.0
A Guide to Reclaiming the Commons

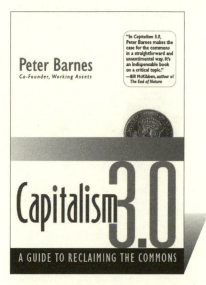

Our current version of capitalism—the corporate, globalized version 2.0—is rapidly squandering our shared heritage. It is driving us headlong into social, economic, and environmental collapse. Barnes proposes an alternative to our current self-destructive path: Capitalism 3.0, an update that includes innovative features to protect the commons while preserving the basic processes that have made capitalism such an effective economic operating system. *Capitalism 3.0* offers viable solutions to some of our most pressing economic, environmental, and social concerns.

"Reading Capitalism 3.0 *is like putting on a new pair of glasses. It is clearly written, provocative, and fresh."*
    —**Michael Pollan, author of** *The Omnivore's Dilemma*

Hardcover, 216 pages, ISBN 978-1-57675-361-3

BK® Berrett–Koehler Publishers, Inc.
San Francisco, *www.bkconnection.com*   **800.929.2929**

Edited by Peter Barnes

Jonathan Rowe

Our Common Wealth
The Hidden Economy That Makes Everything Else Work

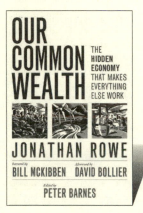

A huge part of our economy is invisible, invaluable, and under siege. This is "the commons," a term that denotes everything we share. Jonathan Rowe illuminates the scale and value of the commons, its symbiotic relationship with the rest of our economy, and its importance to our personal and planetary well-being. He unifies many seemingly disparate struggles—against pollution, excessive development, corporate marketing to children, and more—with the force of this powerful idea. And he calls for new institutions that create a durable balance between the commons and the profit-seeking side of our economy.

"This elegant book...will change the way you think about economic, environmental, and social problems and how to solve them."
—James Fallows, national correspondent, *The Atlantic*

Paperback, 144 pages, ISBN 978-1-60994-833-7
PDF ebook, ISBN 978-1-60994-834-4

BK° Berrett–Koehler Publishers, Inc.
San Francisco, *www.bkconnection.com*   800.929.2929

Berrett–Koehler
Publishers

Berrett-Koehler is an independent publisher dedicated to an ambitious mission: *Creating a World That Works for All*.

We believe that to truly create a better world, action is needed at all levels—individual, organizational, and societal. At the individual level, our publications help people align their lives with their values and with their aspirations for a better world. At the organizational level, our publications promote progressive leadership and management practices, socially responsible approaches to business, and humane and effective organizations. At the societal level, our publications advance social and economic justice, shared prosperity, sustainability, and new solutions to national and global issues.

A major theme of our publications is "Opening Up New Space." Berrett-Koehler titles challenge conventional thinking, introduce new ideas, and foster positive change. Their common quest is changing the underlying beliefs, mindsets, institutions, and structures that keep generating the same cycles of problems, no matter who our leaders are or what improvement programs we adopt.

We strive to practice what we preach—to operate our publishing company in line with the ideas in our books. At the core of our approach is stewardship, which we define as a deep sense of responsibility to administer the company for the benefit of all of our "stakeholder" groups: authors, customers, employees, investors, service providers, and the communities and environment around us.

We are grateful to the thousands of readers, authors, and other friends of the company who consider themselves to be part of the "BK Community." We hope that you, too, will join us in our mission.

A BK Currents Book

This book is part of our BK Currents series. BK Currents books advance social and economic justice by exploring the critical intersections between business and society. Offering a unique combination of thoughtful analysis and progressive alternatives, BK Currents books promote positive change at the national and global levels. To find out more, visit www.bkconnection.com.

Berrett–Koehler
Publishers

A community dedicated to creating
a world that works for all

Dear Reader,

Thank you for picking up this book and joining our worldwide community of Berrett-Koehler readers. We share ideas that bring positive change into people's lives, organizations, and society.

To welcome you, we'd like to offer you a free e-book. You can pick from among twelve of our bestselling books by entering the promotional code **BKP92E** here: http://www.bkconnection.com/welcome.

When you claim your free e-book, we'll also send you a copy of our e-newsletter, the *BK Communiqué*. Although you're free to unsubscribe, there are many benefits to sticking around. In every issue of our newsletter you'll find

• A free e-book
• Tips from famous authors
• Discounts on spotlight titles
• Hilarious insider publishing news
• A chance to win a prize for answering a riddle

Best of all, our readers tell us, "Your newsletter is the only one I actually read." So claim your gift today, and please stay in touch!

Sincerely,

Charlotte Ashlock
Steward of the BK Website

Questions? Comments? Contact me at bkcommunity@bkpub.com.

MIX
From responsible
sources
FSC® C113845

Certified

Corporation
bcorporation.net